THE COMPLETE GUIDE TO LEONBERGERS

Vanessa Richie

Publication Data

Vanessa Richie

The Complete Guide to Leonbergers – First edition.

Summary: "Successfully raising a Leonberger dog from puppy to old age" – Provided by publisher.

ISBN: 978-1-954288-48-5

[1. Leonbergers – Non-Fiction] I. Title.

Design by Sorin Rădulescu
First paperback edition, 2022

TABLE OF CONTENTS

PART 2
Adopting and the Early Days with Your Leonberger . .

PART 3
Training and Activities

CHAPTER 10

House-training

CHAPTER 11

Training Your Leonberger

PART 4
Taking Care of Your Leonberger

INTRODUCTION

The Leonberger looks intimidating, but it is one of the sweetest dogs you'll ever encounter. Reaching between 90 and 150 pounds and 25 to 31.5 inches tall, this is a dog that will easily take up the entire couch, but it is not the kind of dog that will want to sit down without a good bit of exercise first. Unlike a lot of larger dogs, Leonbergers have energy to spare, making them great dogs for people who like to be active. This is a breed that is used to help with therapy work because Leonbergers are strong and calm.

This is one of the first known examples of a dog that was intentionally bred for a specific purpose, making it similar to today's designer breeds. Three parent breeds were used to create this gentle, loving dog: the Newfoundland, Saint Bernard (long-haired), and Great Pyrenees. All three of these breeds are large and acclimated to really cold climates. Leonbergers do not do well in warmer climates because of their thicker coats. Also, some of them may drool a bit more than others, thanks to their Saint Bernard roots.

Since it is a higher energy large dog, this isn't a breed that should be adopted because you think it will be easy to train. Leonbergers tend to be mischievous, and young or untrained dogs can make quite a mess. Given that they are prolific shedders, this is not a breed for people who want a pristine home or who don't have a lot of patience. However, Leonbergers are great family dogs because they seem to have nearly boundless patience with children and are incredibly loyal. That said, when they are young, you will definitely want to keep an eye on them with small children as young Leonbergers don't realize just how big they are and may accidentally hurt smaller kids.

Sadly, Leonbergers have the same short life span as many other large-dog breeds, reaching only about eight or nine years of age. Under the right conditions, your Leonberger may live a little longer than that. They start to slow down by six or seven, and at that age, your Leonberger will be much happier to cuddle up with you after far less activity.

This book is divided into four sections:

- **PART 1 – GETTING TO KNOW THE LEONBERGER**

  This section provides basic information about the breed, including a brief history, a description of the breed's appearance, and their characteristics so that you can determine if this is the right kind of dog for you and your household.

- **PART 2 – ADOPTING AND THE EARLY DAYS WITH YOUR LEONBERGER**

  These chapters will help you plan for your Leonberger's arrival and help you map your first month with your newest family member.

- **PART 3 – TRAINING AND ACTIVITIES**

  Here is where we will help you understand the challenges you will face, as well as provide the knowledge you need to help you be successful in your training.

- **PART 4 – TAKING CARE OF YOUR LEONBERGER**

  These chapters cover how to take care of your Leonberger's health, the breed's hereditary ailments, and canine ailments that come with age.

PART 1

GETTING TO KNOW THE LEONBERGER

CHAPTER 1

Is the Leonberger Right for You?

The appearance of the Leonberger is similar to a very small lion; these dogs are absolutely enormous. Given their size, the large amount of fur, higher energy, and intelligence, this is a breed that requires a certain type of home and family. With the right family, though, they are fantastic dogs that will guard the home and thrive as a highly entertaining part of the family.

Important Considerations

> "
>
> *Leos make wonderful family dogs and can really adapt to many lifestyles as long as you have the time and attention to devote to their physical and emotional well-being. My Leos love people and other animals. On any given day at the farm, we have 8–10 dogs (and often more people than I can count) and the Leos love the attention and companionship that all of that offers. At home, I also have a small dog and cats, and the Leos love them too.*
>
> ELLIE ADAMS
> *Rocky Ford Leonbergers*
>
> "

One of the reasons that people love well-established breeds is that you pretty much know what you are going to get, regardless of the age of the dog. Socialization can help minimize some behaviors, but older dog breeds are largely set in their ways. The usual temperament of the Leonberger is good, but if untrained or unsocialized, you could have a very difficult, incredibly large dog. Here's what you can expect from your Leonberger.

WHAT'S GREAT ABOUT LEONBERGERS

Another member of the family	These dogs love their families and want to spend their time enjoying being around everyone. Their patience with kids and others is phenomenal.
A fantastic exercise buddy	While you do need to make sure Leonbergers don't overheat, there really isn't an activity that this dog can't join in some way. With their energy levels, they can go on long jogs with you. They also love swimming, playing in the snow, and hiking. If you are game for it, you probably won't have to ask your dog twice—just be ready with a large bowl of water when you are done.
Polite and gentle	This breed is known for being incredibly gentle and patient, learning quickly not to jump on others and to help make others comfortable around them, even if the dog does look intimidating.
A great guard dog	Even though they are lovable, affable dogs, Leonbergers have a deep bark that is scary to people who don't know them. They aren't aggressive, but they have been described as sensibly protective.
A sensitive dog	One of the things that people really love about Leonbergers is that they are sensitive to emotions. This is definitely something to keep in mind as they can try to intercede in arguments. They don't attack but will non-aggressively try to get people to calm down, especially if there is shouting.

WHY A LEONBERGER MAY NOT BE RIGHT FOR YOU

Not a first dog	Between the breed's size, intellect, and energy, if you haven't had a dog before, do not start with a Leonberger. These dogs require patience, firmness, and a healthy approach to training. This makes them a bad choice for people who have no history of training a dog in the home.
An incredibly large dog	Big dogs are more expensive and have shorter life spans. This is also a dog that loves people, so he will probably lean on your leg with his large frame to show love, but it can be a lot of weight against your leg because of the dog's size.
Strong prey drive	They may be gentle giants toward people, but Leonbergers will try to chase smaller animals.

WHY A LEONBERGER MAY NOT BE RIGHT FOR YOU

Potential for stubbornness	Bringing an intelligent canine into your home comes with the risk of having a stubborn dog. Training with positive, firm, consistent methods is the way to get around this, but you also need to be patient.
Prolific shedders	Though experts say Leonbergers have two primary shedding periods every year, you will feel like the two shedding seasons are the first half of the year and the second half of the year. These dogs require frequent grooming to remove tangles, debris, and dead hair.
Potential behavior issues	When they are young, Leonbergers need to be trained early to keep them from jumping up on people because they grow fast, and that energy level kicks in early. They can be exuberant, rowdy, and destructive without proper training, something that is a much more serious issue with larger dogs.
Potential aggression without proper training	Beyond their energy levels, without proper socialization and training, Leonbergers can be more aggressive toward strangers and other pets. It's a pretty easy problem to avoid, but if you rescue an adult, you will need to be more cautious when meeting people and other animals.
Hard to find	Leonbergers are hard to find, and when you do find one, it is usually very expensive to acquire.
A few serious health concerns	Like all established breeds, Leonbergers have some known genetic issues, and a few of them are very serious. While this is generally a healthy breed (especially given their size), there are some health concerns that you should know before you bring one into your home.

Adult Versus Puppy

The final question to ask yourself before you settle on a particular breed is whether you should get an adult or a puppy. The answer varies based on the individual or family. Probably the biggest consideration is their size because you have to be more aware as puppies grow into adults. You will need to regularly adjust collars and crates to accommodate your growing puppy. Adult dogs will require more monitoring when around other people and pets until you know their personality and temperament. They are a good-natured breed, but without proper training and socialization, their size can make them more dangerous than smaller dogs, so you need to be prepared to quickly earn your new dog's respect and be very mindful of them for that first year.

Beyond their size, there are a number of other factors that you need to weigh to decide if you want to rescue or adopt a Leonberger. Here are some considerations to help you determine which age dog is a better fit for your home.

Bringing Home an Adult Leonberger

As mentioned earlier, you need to be careful and really consider if you can handle adopting an adult; if the dog is not properly trained, life can turn into a real struggle because of your new canine's stubbornness. Since Leonbergers are so big, they can also be rough, even if they don't mean to be. They can also be destructive if they don't get enough mental and physical exercise. You need to plan to start training from the moment you bring home the dog because even if your new Leonberger has been trained, you still have to prove you are someone who should be listened to. Essentially, you have to prove you are a worthy leader, just like you would at a job, and that means being patient, positive, and kind, along with being firm and consistent.

If you have young children at home, you will need to watch your dog closely and make sure he has a positive reaction to kids, especially if you don't know the dog's history. You should also be careful about introducing a Leonberger to other pets, although most Leonbergers tend to warm up to other animals fairly quickly. Note that if the animals are smaller, he may chase them, as discussed earlier.

Adult dogs can give you more immediate gratification. You don't have to go through the sleepless nights that come with a new puppy. The odds are also that you aren't going

HELPFUL TIP
Leonberger Club of America (LCA)

Founded in 1985, the Leonberger Club of America (LCA) is the largest Leonberger breed club in the US. The LCA is governed by a board of directors, offering a host of events and shows throughout the year. The LCA also publishes a quarterly edition of the "LeoLetter: Great Dogs, Great People," where you can read about club news and stay up to date on happenings with the breed. For more information about the club, visit www.leonbergerclubofamerica.com.

to be starting from the beginning with house-training.

Additionally, adult dogs are awake during the day a lot more than puppies, and while it may take your new dog a bit longer to warm up to you, you can still bond much faster with an adult.

Finally, one of the biggest benefits of acquiring an adult dog is that it will already be its full size. There is no need for guessing how big your dog will grow to be, and that makes it easier to purchase the appropri-

Photo Courtesy of Isabelle Cotelle

ate-sized gear and supplies right from the start.

The following is a list of questions to consider when adopting an adult Leonberger:

- **Can you properly dog-proof your home before the dog arrives?**

You can't simply bring a dog into your home, whether an adult or a puppy, and let him run around unchecked. To be sure he learns the rules of the house before he is allowed to roam freely, you will need to have a safe, dedicated space for your new dog. (Details of how to dog-proof your home are discussed in Chapter 5.)

- **Do you have pets that will be affected by a new dog?**

Leonbergers are likely to get along just fine with any dog—and probably cats—but you will still want to be very careful since you don't know the dog's history with other animals. This introduction should take place over the first couple of months. Introducing the animals in a neutral territory will show you what to expect when your Leonberger and your current dog(s) are together on a permanent basis. Even if they appear to be compatible, you still need to keep them apart for a while. This will ensure your new Leonberger understands that the other dogs are part of the pack and are not a threat to him.

You will need to be aware of how your other dog(s) reacts as well. Even if your current dog is very friendly, you will still want to be careful when introducing the two animals and allowing them to interact in your home.

- **What is the dog's health history?**

A complete health record for a rescue Leonberger may not be available, but it is likely you will find a dog that has already been spayed or neutered as well as chipped. Unless you adopt a Leonberger with health issues, which should be disclosed by the rescue organization (if known), rescues tend to be less costly than puppies at their first vet visit. In other words, for the first few years, your Leonberger's health-care visits should not be too expensive.

Bringing Home a Leonberger Puppy

Puppies are a major time investment, and a dog as intelligent, large, and energetic as the Leonberger will make some aspects of raising a puppy that much harder. How much time can you devote to a puppy's care? Will you be able to deal with an excitable puppy that has everything to learn and quickly becomes a puppy in a very large body?

A puppy will be a better fit if you can put in dedicated time for training and socializing before the dog becomes set in his ways. If you have other pets at home, a puppy is definitely a better choice than an adult because he is young and can be trained to follow your rules. (The exception would be if you find an adult that is already well-socialized.)

*Photo Courtesy
of Jarek Zieliński*

When determining whether or not a Leonberger puppy is a good fit for your home, ask yourself:

- **How much time do you have available for training and socialization?**

All puppies are a lot of work, starting with the moment the puppy enters your care. While the Leonberger's temperament is fairly predictable, how you train and socialize your puppy will affect every aspect of the dog's adult life. Training and socializing can take up a large chunk of time in the beginning, but both are absolutely essential for raising a healthy, well-mannered Leonberger.

- **Are you able to show firmness and consistency when training?**

From the very start, you have to establish yourself and your family as the ones in charge; your Leonberger must understand his place in the family hierarchy. You will need to be patient and consistent with your training, no matter how frustrated you become or how cute those puppy eyes are. All intelligent dogs have a streak of stubbornness!

- **Do you have the time, energy, and budget to puppy-proof your home?**

The preparation for your puppy's arrival begins long before he first sets foot in your house. Puppy-proofing your home is as time-consuming as child-proofing your home. If you do not have the time for this, then you should consider getting an adult dog instead of a puppy. (Details of how to puppy-proof your home are discussed in Chapter 6.)

You will receive records about the puppy and the puppy's parents, which will make it easier to identify any health problems your Leonberger might experience in the future. This makes it considerably easier to keep your puppy healthy and to spot potential issues before they become major problems.

Some people find it easier to bond with puppies than with adult dogs. A young puppy may be nervous in a new home, but most adjust quickly because they are predisposed to enjoying the company of those around them.

CHAPTER 2

Breed History of the Leonberger

There are a lot of things that are unique about the Leonberger, and that remains true when it comes to their history. Over 100 years before designer dogs were all the rage, the Leonberger was one of the few (if not the only) breeds that were intentionally bred based on the characteristics of other dogs. The Leonberger became an incredibly important breed following major events in Europe during the 20th century. Today, these dogs are well-loved, even if they are incredibly difficult to find.

Photo Courtesy of Alitza Vagenknechtova

The Leonberg Crest and Germanic Heritage

Leonberg is a German town near the city of Stuttgart, and the breed originates from this town. There are a lot of stories about how and why Heinrich Essig began trying to breed a new dog. The story that is most often believed is that Essig wanted to have a dog to represent Leonberg. In 1846, he began breeding St. Bernards and Landseer Newfoundlands to create a dog that would be symbolic of his home city in the less popular Baden-Wurttemberg state. The city's crest and coat of arms included a lion, and Essig wanted to breed a canine that closely matched the crest.

Essig seems to have gotten the idea of breeding a lion from two dogs that he already owned, a white and black Newfoundland and a long-haired St. Bernard. These dogs were the foundation for the first four Leonberger generations, but it is believed that at some point during those early days of the new breed, Essig added a Pyrenees mountain dog to the mix. Much of what he did was not recorded, and he closely guarded the breeding program from others.

One of the First Intended Breeds

Designer dogs are canines that are intentionally bred from several established breeds, with the Labradoodle (a Labrador and Poodle mix) being perhaps the best well known. Usually, this kind of breeding is done to try to obtain a dog with particular characteristics.

The primary difference between the designer breeds of today and the Leonberger is that a lot more is known about intentional breeds today, and they are often created by several breeders at around the same time. DNA on the dogs today indicates that there were other breeds included in the early days of the breed, but the data isn't accurate enough to determine what those other breeds were. By comparison, breeds today are tracked

Photo Courtesy of Isabelle Cotelle

FUN FACT
Musicians'
Best Friend

Two European composers notably owned Leonbergers: Richard Wagner, the German composer known for his operas, and Sergei Rachmaninoff, a Russian composer and accomplished pianist.

by a much larger group of people and monitored to ensure that a new breed is healthy.

The Leonberger was primarily Essig's project, and he did not want other people to be able to replicate his process. Luckily, Essig told several members of his family about the breeding program, particularly his niece, Marie, who spent a lot of time working in the kennels.

Following Essig's death in 1889, his family took over breeding the dogs that he loved. Just a few years later, in 1895, Albert Kull began recording the standards for the family's new breed. This included details about what they could do as a more energetic, large dog. As Europe prepared to enter World War I, this became a significant hazard to the breed, bringing them near the brink of extinction.

Keeping the Breed Alive

The ramifications of World War I went well beyond the toll of human life. Many animals were employed during the battles, and it brought many animals to the brink of extinction—and in some cases, they did not make it beyond the war (carrier pigeons went extinct in 1914). It is estimated that people employed 16 million animals between 1914 and 1918.

Leonbergers were unique in that they had a lot of potential uses during the war, from pulling ammunition carts to working with the soldiers. There weren't a great number of them when the war began, so their numbers were quickly decimated as they became casualties of the war.

As the war reached the Leonberg area of Germany, breeders were killed or fled the area, leaving the dogs to largely fend for themselves. The reason that the breed survived was that a group of Leonbergers ensured that there were enough dogs to continue breeding as the war drew to a close. According to some reports, there were only five breeding Leonbergers left at the end of the war.

By the time World War II started, the breed had largely recovered. Albert Kienzle was one of the primary breeders who managed to keep the breed alive following World War II. He and some of the other breeders began to shrink the size of the breed by a few centimeters in height. This was likely as a result of the breed failing in other areas, such as the US, because the breed was too hard to care for during severe economic times. The breed continued to survive in France, but the French kept dogs closer to the original size for a long time after the Germans revised the breeding standards.

The Modern-Day Leonberger

The original Leonbergers did not get a great reception, with some people saying the new breed was just a "Saint Bernard Wannabe." For a long time, they were not recognized by breeder organizations and dog shows. However, following World War II, people from other countries seemed to take an interest in the breed, with one British soldier trading 10 bars of soap for a single Leonberger.

It wasn't until the 1970s and 1980s that the breed really started to make a comeback and received a lot more attention. A small group of Leonberger enthusiasts began to actively work to re-estab-

Photo Courtesy of Brian and Leah Peters

lish the breed and re-introduce it to the different breeder organizations. They were successful, so there are now thousands of Leonbergers around the world today.

CHAPTER 3
Leonberger Attributes and Temperament

Leonbergers are fantastic dogs, providing protection, an exercise companion, and a highly entertaining family member. They also come with a lot of work because of their size and intelligence. This is decidedly not a good dog for people who haven't trained a dog before since there is a lot of work that comes with the Leonberger, including managing a thick coat and keeping the dog's boredom in check. In other words, Leonbergers will keep you on your toes and entertained.

Photo Courtesy of Leon Gerrits

A Lion in Shape and a Teddy Bear in Personality

> *Leonbergers can be wonderful family dogs, but you must be prepared to have a 120–170-pound dog underfoot all of the time. They will follow you around the house and want to lie beside you or on you and have no knowledge of personal space. Leonbergers want to be with their family ALL THE TIME and are not a breed that can be left outside or be gated in a separate area of your house. You have to be able to spend time with them every day, loving on them, taking them for a short walk, training them, or taking them with you for a car ride.*
>
> SUE HERMAN
> *Water's Edge Leonbergers*

Bred to look like a lion, Leonbergers are massive teddy bears in a dog's body. They are affectionate, protective, and loving.

A Large Frame

Though the breed today has been intentionally bred to be somewhat smaller than the original versions, the Leonberger remains an incredibly large dog. Males tend to be slightly larger than females, standing at about 31 inches to their shoulders compared to the female's 19 inches. Their heads are massive, like the two original parent breeds. They have been used as working dogs, so they are muscular under two thick double coats of fur. They are also barrel-chested under all the fuzz, which helped them work in harsh conditions during their earlier history.

This is decidedly not a dog for apartments or small homes that don't have a yard. They not only take up a lot of space, but they are considerably more energetic than the average large dog.

The Noble Face and Demeanor

A Leonberger's large head is like that of a lion, with a regal-looking, rectangular face. The Leonberger face is mostly black until the dog gets older,

Photo Courtesy
of Aare Ööpik

and it is free of wrinkles. They have brown eyes that look wise, something that can fool those who don't know how mischievous the breed can be when bored. They have triangular ears that fold over and hang down the sides of their heads.

HISTORICAL FACT
A Royal Companion

Leonbergers are part of the Working Group and are descended from large, hardy working breeds such as Newfoundlands and Saint Bernards. However, these gentle giants were initially intended to serve as regal companions for European royalty. Royal Leonberger owners included Tsar Alexander II, Napoleon III, and King Edward the VII. So, while these dogs can pull their weight as working dogs, their calm and gentle demeanor is an equally compelling facet of the breed.

A Working Dog Coat

Leonbergers have a thick double coat. Their fur is medium length and is resistant to water (something that was necessary in snowy, rainy climates). That luxurious coat is not as soft as it looks, but the undercoat is incredibly soft, more like puppy fur. Males have more fur on their head and neck, similar to the way male lions have manes, and they have longer coats than female Leonbergers. Though they have a lot of fur, they are not styled like other dogs, so you won't need to cut their fur like dogs such as the Poodle.

Temperament

Born of two breeds that are known for being gentle and mild-mannered most of the time, Leonbergers are patient and even-tempered. Today they are largely family pets and companions, a role that is nearly perfect for them, as long as they are properly trained. They are sensitive to the emotions of the people around them.

A Gentle Giant

The Leonberger is the archetypal gentle giant. These dogs are able to put up with the antics of a toddler with the kind of patience that parents can envy. They also love the people they live with and want to be with them as much as possible. Happy to just be with their family after a busy day, they are pretty easy to entertain and are very capable of entertaining you.

Friendly, Loyal, and Affectionate

Given their patience, it shouldn't come as a surprise that Leonbergers are a largely friendly breed that can be very affectionate with the people they know well. While they won't give the same kind of attention and affection to strangers, they also aren't going to snap and act particularly suspicious, like the German Shepherd, Doberman, or Rottweiler. However, they can be protective if they feel it is the right response to a situation.

They are also kid-friendly, though you definitely need to keep an eye on them with smaller children, as they may get very excited and fail to realize just how big they are. They are generally fine with other pets, though you will need to be careful during the introductions. What really helps them to meld well with nearly any family is the fact that they love to please their people, something that is easy since they can join in on many different activities.

A High-Energy Dog

Most people choose large dogs because they tend to be either couch potatoes or guard dogs. The Leonberger doesn't fall into either of these categories. Instead, this is a large breed that loves to swim, run, and be incredibly active. They are far more agile than their size suggests. This means you have a lot of ways to tire them out to keep them out of trouble.

Photo Courtesy
of Lili Costagliola

Training Is Essential, Especially with Smaller Animals

Leonbergers don't seem to realize just how big and strong they are. Without proper training, they can knock people over and do a lot of damage. They also have a higher prey drive than their looks would suggest, so they can be a bit of a menace with smaller animals in the home, including cats. With training, they will be fine with cats, rabbits, and other small animals, but you will need to be patient with them to ensure that they love your other pets as much as they love you—or at least practice the same kind of patience with other animals that they have with young children.

Photo Courtesy of Ian Sears

Breed Standards

Only Leonberg is allowed to make changes to the standards of the breed. Other organizations do keep their own standards, but the official standards are set by the place where the dogs were first bred. The Federation Cynologique Internationale tracks the standards on their website **(http://www.fci.be/nomenclature/Standards/145g02-en.pdf)**. If you are interested in registering your dog for shows, you can reference the standards. Any breed that is outside of these standards is less likely to be accepted into shows.

PART 2

ADOPTING AND THE EARLY
DAYS WITH YOUR LEONBERGER

CHAPTER 4
Finding Your Leonberger

Leonbergers tend to be very expensive to adopt. Rescuing an adult is far less costly, typically averaging about $300. Puppies bought from good breeders start at $1,500 and can go up to several thousand dollars. They are also expensive to care for at home because they need large everything, from crates to beds.

Ways to Get a Leonberger

This chapter is broken into two primary sections: rescuing a Leonberger and adopting a Leonberger. Typically, people rescue an adult, and they adopt a puppy.

Photo Courtesy of Leon Gerrits

- Dog rescues are one of the most reliable ways to get a healthy adult Leonberger. The rescuers tend to go above and beyond to ensure the health of the dog.
- Shelters are usually not dedicated to any one breed. However, that doesn't mean you can't find a Leonberger or a dog that has a lot of Leonberger genetics and that lovable temperament.

While you can get puppies from both rescue organizations and shelters, it is more likely that you will find a puppy at one of the following sources:

- Breeders are the most reliable source for purebred dogs, but you have to be careful. Puppy mills focus on producing as many dogs as possible for the lowest cost. They are far less likely to do any testing and screening, so their dogs are more likely to have genetic problems.
- Pet stores may get their dogs from a puppy mill. They also aren't likely to get their dogs from a great breeder (breeders who really take care of their dogs are far more likely to be picky about who adopts their puppies).

You can find rescued puppies from puppy mills and pet stores at a dog rescue or pet shelter. You can also get a great adult dog from a breeder, especially if a breeder takes one of their dogs back from a client who did not follow the contract. Sometimes people have to surrender their dogs, and breeders often prefer to have their dogs returned to them so they can find another good home.

To find your perfect Leonberger, make sure to check multiple avenues unless you want a puppy, in which case a breeder is probably your best bet.

Rescuing a Leonberger

Considering the fact that this is not a well-known breed, you will have a much harder time rescuing a purebred Leonberger. The following are several websites that can help you find a Leonberger to adopt:

- Leonberger Rescue Pals (https://lrpals.org)
- Gentle Giants Rescue and Adoptions (http://www.gentlegiantsrescue.com/leonbergers.htm)
- Rescue Pledge (https://www.rescuepledge.org/adopt/leonbergers)

You may also be able to find dogs in your region, so it could be worth your time to spend an hour or so looking for a dog closer to you. If that doesn't work out, you can also contact Leonberger breeders to see if they have had any of their puppies returned that are at least two years old. That way, the breeders will have a better understanding of the dog and its person-ality, and they will be able to answer any future questions you might have.

Keep in mind the following questions when adopting a Leonberger:

- What is the reason the dog was surrendered?
- Did the dog have any health issues when he arrived?
- Do they know how the dog was treated by the previous family? What kind of training was he given? Was he mistreated? And was he socialized?
- How many homes has the dog experienced?
- What kind of veterinary care did the dog receive? Are there records that confirm this?
- Will the dog require extra medical attention based on known or sus-pected problems?
- Is the dog house-trained?
- How well does the dog react to strangers while walking in unfamiliar areas?
- Does the dog tend to be aggressive or guard his food when eating?
- How does the dog react to children and to other dogs and pets?
- Does the dog have any known allergies?
- Does the dog have any known dietary restrictions?
- If there are problems with the dog after adoption, will the organiza-tion take him back?

Types of Rescues

It is incredibly unlikely you will find a Leonberger in a shelter or typical rescue place, though you may be able to find a Leonberger mix. However, you almost certainly will not be able to get documentation about the dog's breeding, training, and socialization. Also, the temperament will be far less predictable than a purebred, as the dog could take after any other breed that helps make up the genetics.

Rescue and Shelter Adoption Requirements

Adopting an adult is significantly different from adopting a puppy. Since the dogs have already been to at least one home prior to being brought into a rescue, the more diligent rescues want to make sure that their dogs go to a home that is willing and able to take care of their dogs, minimizing the likelihood that he will be returned. When a rescue is dedicated to a breed, they will have different, more breed-specific methods of handling and taking care of the dog. There are no rescue requirements or standards that apply everywhere. Some require home visits, though this tends to be fairly rare. Others have set requirements for what you have to do within a set amount of time after your dog goes home with you. In the US, many of the shelter requirements are based on state laws about what people with pets must do. The website NomNom has created a page that details the requirements for those living in the US at Pet

Photo Courtesy of Sandy Geldhof

Adoption Laws by State (https://www.nomnomnow.com/learn/article/pet-adoption-laws-by-state).

With a breed like the Leonberger, you may have more success with asking breeders if they have an adult or returned dog instead of looking for the rare rescues that specialize in Leonbergers. Many breeders require puppies or dogs to be returned to them if the adopting family is unable to continue to take care of the dog, so they may have one or two adults they are willing to adopt out. Their requirements for adopting a returned dog will be different from adopting a dog from a rescue.

Choosing a Leonberger Breeder and Puppy

> *Do your research! Ensure that the breeder you choose completes all the required health tests on their breeding dogs, provides a contract with the puppy, and allows you to visit. I always encourage puppy buyers to find a breeder that they can work with and that will support them throughout the life of the puppy.*
>
> ERIN ANDERSEN
> *High Hopes Newfoundlands and Leonbergers*

Finding a responsible breeder is the best thing you can do for your puppy because good breeders work only with healthy Leonberger parents, which reduces the odds of serious genetic health issues. Leonbergers typically cost between $1,200 and $5,000, so you are looking at a pretty large spread in cost, depending on where the breeder is located and how long they've been established. While cost is important, it is far more important to understand the breeder to ensure you get a healthy dog.

Always take the time to do your research before moving forward. Although breeders for Leonbergers are largely reputable, you also might run across an individual who is more interested in making a lot of money than in caring for the dogs. The goal is to locate breeders who are willing to answer ALL of your questions patiently and thoroughly. They should show as much love for their Leonbergers as they expect you to show for your new puppy; their goal should be to locate good homes for all of their animals.

It is a particularly good sign if you find a breeder who posts pictures and information about the dog's parents, documents the progress of the mother's pregnancy, and shares descriptions of all vet visits. The best breeders will also stay in contact with you and answer any questions that might arise after you take the puppy home. Taking an active interest in what happens to the puppies in their new homes shows that breeders care a great deal about each individual dog.

You also want to find a breeder who is willing to talk about problems that might develop with your Leonberger. Good breeders will ensure the adopting family is capable of properly socializing and training their Leonberger.

It is likely that your conversation with each breeder will last about an hour. Make sure you take careful notes during every interview. If a breeder does not have time to talk when you call and isn't willing to call you back—cross them off your list!

The following are some questions to consider when researching breeders:

- Ask if you can visit in person. The answer should always be yes, and if it isn't, you don't need to ask anything further. Thank the breeder and hang up. Even if the breeder is located in a different state, they should always allow you to visit their facility.

- Ask about the health tests and certifications breeders have for their puppies. (These points are detailed further in the next section, so make sure to check off the available tests and certifications with every breeder.) If they don't have all of the tests and certifications, remove the breeder from your list of considerations.

- Make sure the breeder takes care of the initial health requirements, particularly shots, for each puppy from the first few weeks of birth through the dog's early months. Vaccinations and worming typically start at around six weeks of age and should be continued every three weeks. By the time your puppy is old enough to come home with you, he should be well into the first phase of these procedures or be completely finished with these important health care needs.

- Ask if the puppy is required to be spayed or neutered before reaching a certain age.

- Inquire whether or not the breeder is part of a Leonberger organization or group.

- Ask about the first phases of your puppy's life, such as how the breeder will take care of the puppy before it goes home with you. They should be able to provide a lot of details, and they should not sound irritated by your questioning. They should also explain what training your puppy will receive prior to leaving the facility. It is possible the breeder might start house-training your puppy. If so, ask about the puppy's progress so that you know where to pick up training once your Leonberger reaches your home.

FUN FACT
Leonberger Rescue Pals

Leonberger Rescue Pals is a 501(c)3 founded in 1998 with the approval of the Leonberger Club of America (LCA) board of directors. This rescue program is run by volunteers and foster-based, serving Leonbergers across the United States. Available dogs can be viewed on their website at www.lrpals.org.

- Breeders should be more than happy to help guide you in doing what is best for your dog because they should want their puppies to live happy, healthy lives. You should also be able to rely on any recommendations your breeder makes about taking your puppy home, particularly about the first days living with the puppy.

- Ask how many varieties of dogs the breeder manages in one year and how many sets of parent dogs they own. Mother dogs should have some downtime between pregnancies before producing another litter. Learn about breeders' standard operations to be sure they take care of the parents and treat them as valuable family members—not strictly as a way to make money.

- Ask about aggression in the puppy's parents and find out if there are other dogs in the breeder's home. While a puppy's temperament is more malleable than an adult's, some exposure to other breeds might make it easier when integrating the puppy into a home that already has dogs. Aggression isn't a normal problem for Leonbergers, but if you have smaller animals in your home, this will be important to know.

Contracts and Guarantees

Breeder contracts and guarantees are meant to protect the puppies as much as they are meant to protect you. If a breeder has a contract, make sure you read through it completely and are willing to meet all of the requirements prior to signing. Contracts tend to be fairly easy to understand and to comply with, but you should be aware of all the facts before you agree to anything. Signing the contract indicates you are serious about committing to giving your puppy the best care possible and to meeting the minimum care requirements set forth by the breeder.

A contract may state the breeder will retain the puppy's original registration papers, although you will receive a copy of the papers too.

If a family does not meet all requirements as stated in the contract, it is the breeder's responsibility to remove the puppy from the family. These are the dogs some breeders offer for adoption.

A guarantee states the kind of health care the puppy is to receive once it leaves the breeder's facility. This typically includes details about the dog's

Photo Courtesy of Ashley Cote

current health and the recommendations for the next steps in the puppy's health care. Guarantees may also provide veterinary schedules to ensure that the health care started by the breeder is continued by the new puppy parent. In the event that a major health concern surfaces, the puppy will be returned to the breeder.

The contract will also explain what is not covered by the guarantee. A guarantee tends to be quite long (sometimes longer than the contract), and you should also read it thoroughly before signing it.

Leonberger contracts usually include a requirement that the dog is spayed or neutered once it reaches maturity (typically six months). The contract may also contain requirements for naming your puppy (if you would like more information about naming requirements, check out the American Kennel Club for details about contracts), details of the puppy's health, and a stipulation regarding what will happen if you can no longer take care of the animal. Information concerning the steps that will be taken if the new owner is negligent or abusive to the dog is also included in the contract.

Health Tests and Certifications

A healthy puppy requires healthy parents and a clean genetic history, which is a bit more difficult to guarantee in a Leonberger due to the history of this breed. A conscientious breeder keeps extensive records for each puppy and its parents. You should review each of the parents' complete histories to understand what traits your puppy is likely to inherit. Pay attention to temperament, learning traits, attachment issues, and any other personality traits you consider important. You can request these documents be sent to you electronically, or you can pick them up when you visit the breeder in person.

It might be time-consuming to review the breeder's information for each parent, but it is always well worth the time. The more you know about the parents, the better prepared you will be for your puppy.

There are a number of tests that must be run on Leonberger parents to make sure that the puppies are unlikely to have the known genetic issues associated with the breed:

- Hip Evaluation
- Elbow Evaluation
- Ophthalmologist Exam
- Thyroid Evaluation
- LPN1, LPN2, and LPN3 DNA Tests
- LEMP DNA Test

These tests do not guarantee that the puppies won't have problems, but parents who score well on the tests are less likely to pass on genetic issues. Chapter 17 details the health issues that are common to the breed, their symptoms, and potential treatments.

Selecting a Puppy from a Breeder

> *The best way to get a Leonberger that will fit into your family is to tell the breeder or rescue organization what it is you are looking for in a dog. Tell them what your lifestyle is like, your activity level, your interests, and if you plan to do any showing. Then you have to trust them to pick the right puppy for your family. The breeder or rescue organization has spent many, many days (24 hours a day) with these puppies and knows their temperaments and activity levels. They will be able to place the right puppy with you.*
>
> SUE HERMAN
> *Water's Edge Leonbergers*

Selecting your puppy should be done in person. However, if the breeder is willing to share videos and pictures, you can start checking out your puppy immediately after he is born!

You should consider the following steps once you are allowed to visit the puppy in person:

- Assess the group of puppies as a whole. If most or all of the puppies are aggressive or fearful, this is an indication of a problem with the litter or (more likely) the breeder. The following are considered red flags if they are displayed by a majority of the puppies:
  - Tucked tails
  - Shrinking away from people
  - Whimpering when people get close
  - Constant attacking of your hands or feet (beyond pouncing)
- Notice how each puppy plays with the other puppies in the litter. This is a great indicator of how your puppy will react to any pets you already

have at home. If you see problems with the way one puppy plays, this could be a problem later.

FUN FACT
How Popular Are They?

According to the American Kennel Club (AKC), Leonbergers were 93rd most popular out of 201 total breeds registered in 2020. The AKC first recognized Leonbergers in 2010. This breed has maintained an AKC popularity ranking from around 93 to 100 for the past 10 years.

- Notice which puppies greet you first and which puppies hang back to observe you from afar. This lets you know their personality and how likely they are to be laid back later.

- Puppies should not be over or underweight. A swollen stomach is generally a sign of worms or other health problems.

- Puppies should have straight, sturdy legs. Splayed legs can be a sign that there is something wrong.

- Examine the puppy's ears for mites, which will cause a discharge if present. The inside of the ear should be pink, not red or inflamed.

- The eyes should be clear and bright.

- Check the puppy's mouth for pink, healthy-looking gums.

- Pet the puppy to check his coat for the following:
    - Be sure the coat feels thick and full. If breeders have allowed puppies' fur to get matted or dirty, it is an indication they are likely not taking proper care of the animals.
    - Check for fleas and mites by running your hand from the head to the tail, then check under the tail as fleas are more likely to hide there. If mites are present, they may look like dandruff.

- Check the puppy's rump for redness and sores; try to check the puppy's last bowel movement to ensure its firmness.

Pick the puppy that exhibits the personality traits you want in your dog. If you want a forward, friendly, excitable dog, the first puppy to greet you may be the one you choose. If you want a dog that will think things through and let others get more attention, look for a puppy that sits back and observes before approaching you. That initial reaction should be on the puppy's terms as much as your own so that you can determine if the personality matches what you think will fit best in your home.

CHAPTER 5

Preparing Your Budget and Family for Your New Leonberger

Leonbergers are expensive to own. Their size means they need more food, larger equipment, and sturdier and larger toys. The budget for the first year is going to be a lot higher for a Leonberger than for a small or medium-sized dog because that cute puppy is going to quickly outgrow everything much faster than you will expect. You should be prepared to adjust crates, collars, and other equipment so that they aren't too small for your growing puppy. If you get an adult, this won't be a problem—you'll just need to buy the large equipment right from the start.

Part 3 of this book goes into the details of the training and socialization of your Leonberger. Different locations have significantly different costs for different types of obedience and training courses, so if you plan to take your dog to classes, you will need to do some research into the costs in your specific area. Make sure to include that cost in your budget.

This chapter will provide the details for the majority of the costs that you will need to cover to ensure you have all of the items your new pup will need before he arrives and over the first year. Since you can go online and get all of these items, the cost is a lot more predictable.

The rest of this chapter details what you need to do to prepare your family. It is a very exciting time, so before your Leonberger arrives, you want to make sure you have all your ducks in a row.

Planning the First Year's Budget

Whether you get a puppy or an adult dog, the costs are always higher than you initially thought. You will definitely want a budget, which is a good reason to start purchasing supplies a few months in advance. As you buy the items you need, you will begin to formulate an idea of how much money you will spend each month. Many of these items are one-time purchases (or won't need to be bought too often, like a bed), but many other items, like food and treats, will have to be purchased regularly.

The following table will help you plan your budget. Keep in mind the prices are rough estimates and may be significantly different based on your location.

Item	Considerations	Estimated Costs
Crate	You will need two crates: one for the puppy and one for when the puppy grows up. Even a puppy can weigh 36 lbs. at three months. This should be a comfortable space where the puppy will sleep and rest.	Wire crates: Range $60 to $350 Portable crate: Range $35 to $200
Bed	You will probably need two beds: one for the puppy and one for when the pup grows up. This will be placed in the crate.	$10 to $55
Leash	The leash should be short in the beginning because you need to be able to keep your puppy from getting overexcited and running to the end of a long line.	Short leash: $6 to $15 Retractable: $8 to $25
Doggie bags for walks	If you walk at parks, this won't be necessary. For those who don't have daily access to free doggie bags, it is best to purchase packs to ensure you don't run out of bags.	Singles cost less than $1 each. Packs: $4 to $16
Collar	You will likely need two collars: one for the puppy and one for an adult Leonberger.	$10 to $30

Item	Considerations	Estimated Costs
Tags	These will likely be provided by your vet. Find out what information the vet provides for tags, then purchase any tags that are not provided. At a minimum, your Leonberger should have a tag with your address on it in case the pup escapes.	Contact your vet before purchasing to see if the required rabies tags include your contact info.
Puppy food	This one is going to depend on if you make your Leonberger food, if you purchase food, or both. The larger the bag, the higher the cost, but the fewer times you will need to purchase food. You will need to purchase puppy-specific food in the beginning, but that will stop after the second year. Adult dog food is more expensive, particularly for large breeds like the Leonberger.	$9 to $90 per bag
Water and food bowls	These will need to be kept in the puppy's area. If you have other dogs, you will need separate bowls for the puppy.	$10 to $40
Toothbrush/ Toothpaste	You will need to brush your dog's teeth regularly, so plan to use more than one toothbrush during the first year.	$2.50 to $14
Brush	Leonberger coats are hard to maintain, and you should brush them regularly. When they are puppies, brushing offers a great way to bond.	$3.50 to $20
Toys	You definitely want to get your puppy toys for aggressive chewers. You will want to keep getting your Leonberger toys as an adult for play (cost of adult dog toys not included).	$2.00 Packs of toys range from $10 to $20 (easier in the long run as your pup will chew through toys quickly)

Item	Considerations	Estimated Costs
Training treats	You will need those from the beginning and likely won't need to change the treats based on your dog's age; you may need to change treats to keep your dog's interest, though.	$4.50 to $15

You will need to pay attention to when items need to be replaced based on your dog's size. Ultimately, you need to establish a budget for the initial costs, then create a second budget for items that will need to be replaced. Plan to revisit this list at the end of every year for the first two years so you can make sure your dog remains comfortable and happy.

When you contact a vet to plan your first visit with your Leonberger, request a cost estimate for that first year. The cost is substantially different for shots in a major city than in a rural area. Use the rough estimate for shots and other vet costs, and add it to your budget planning for that first year—as well as getting the first vet visit on your calendar.

Instructing Your Children

To help your puppy feel comfortable in his new home, you must make sure your children are careful and gentle with the dog, whether you adopt a puppy or an adult dog. Some kids may try to treat the puppy like a toy; don't let them. Take the time to make sure your children follow all of the "puppy rules" from the very beginning to ensure your puppy feels safe, happy, and isn't accidentally injured.

The following are the Five Golden Rules your children should follow from day one. They apply both to puppies and adult Leonbergers:

- Always be gentle and respectful.

- Do not disturb the puppy during mealtimes.

- Chase is an outside game.

HELPFUL TIP
Are Leonbergers Good with Kids?

Leonbergers are one of the largest dog breeds, but they have a reputation for being gentle and patient, and a well-socialized Leo can be an excellent family dog. However, you may want to exercise caution when introducing an adult Leonberger into a house with small children due to the breed's large size. Never leave children unattended with a dog, especially one new to the family.

- The Leonberger should always remain firmly on the ground. Never pick him up.
- All valuables should be kept out of the puppy's reach.

Since your kids are going to ask why these rules are necessary, the following are some explanations you can use. If necessary, modify the discussion to meet the audience—what you say to a toddler is a lot different than what you should tell a teen about playing with your Leonberger.

Photo Courtesy
of Tim and Amanda Whitaker

Leonbergers tend to love children. You do still need to monitor younger children around them until you know that your dog won't become too excited. Younger children may get a little too rough, and no matter how sturdy Leonbergers are, you don't want your new family member to get hurt by an overexcited child.

Always Be Gentle and Respectful

At no time should anyone be rough with a puppy. It is important to be respectful of your puppy to help him learn to also be respectful toward people and other animals.

This rule must be applied consistently every time your children play with your puppy. Be firm if you see your children getting too excited or rough. You don't want the puppy to get overly excited either because he might end up nipping or biting someone. If he does, it won't be his fault because he is still learning. Make sure your children understand the possible repercussions if they get too rough.

Mealtime

Leonbergers can be protective of their food, especially if you rescue a dog that has previously had to fend for himself. Even if you have a puppy, you don't want him to feel insecure during his mealtime because he will learn to be aggressive whenever he eats. Save yourself, your family, and your dog future problems by making sure mealtime is your dog's time alone. Teach your children their own mealtime is off-limits to the puppy, as well.

No feeding your new dog from the table! From toddlers to teens, this is something you'll really need to emphasize—particularly for foods that your kids don't like. Leonbergers are pets, not garbage disposals, and no amount of cute puppy eyes should be rewarded with scraps from the table. That is a recipe for disaster, as it will get harder to convince your dog to stop begging if other people aren't following your rules.

Chase

Make sure your children understand why a game of chase is perfect for the outdoors (though you'll need to monitor things), but inside the house, chasing is off-limits!

Photo Courtesy of Marita McCahill

Running inside your home gives your Leonberger puppy the impression your home isn't safe for him because he is being chased; it also teaches your puppy that running indoors is allowed, which can be dangerous as the dog gets older and bigger. One of the last things you want to see is your adult Leonberger to go barreling through your home—knocking into people and furniture—because he learned it was fine for him to run in the house when he was a puppy!

Paws on the Ground

It doesn't matter how adorable your Leonberger is—he is a living, breathing creature, and he needs to have his paws on the ground (even though he will quickly grow too big to pick up). You might want to carry your new family member around or play with the pup like a baby, but you and your family will have to resist that urge. The younger your children are, the more difficult it will be for them to understand the difference. It is so tempting to treat the puppy like a baby, but this is uncomfortable and unhealthy for the puppy.

Older children will quickly learn that a puppy's nip or bite hurts a lot more than one would think. Those little teeth are quite sharp, and if a dog nips, he could accidentally be dropped—no one wants that to happen. If your children are never allowed to pick up the puppy, things will be a lot better for everyone involved. Remember, this also applies to you, so don't make things difficult by doing something you constantly tell your children not to do.

Keep Valuables Out of Reach

Your kids will be less than happy if their personal possessions are chewed up by an inquisitive puppy, so teach them to put toys, clothes, and other valuables far out of the puppy's reach.

Preparing Your Current Dogs and Cats

It can be a bit tricky introducing Leonbergers to a home with small animals and cats. Even puppies may want to chase those animals. To get the most well-rounded dog possible, you should start socializing him with your other dogs or pets when he is still a puppy. In most cases, this is a fairly straightforward process as long as your established pets are comfortable with you bringing a new puppy into their home. Even cats may find that they can put up with your Leonberger puppy as long as you can convince your new dog not to chase the cats.

The following are important tasks you should complete when preparing your current pets for the new arrival:

- Set a schedule of activities and the people who will need to participate.
- Preserve your current dog's favorite places and furniture; make sure your current dog's toys and other personal items are not in the puppy's space.
- Have playdates at your home to observe your dog(s) reactions to having an addition to the house.

*Photo Courtesy
of Maryann Zukowski*

Stick to a Schedule

It's essential to have a schedule. Obviously, the puppy is going to receive a lot of attention in the beginning, so you need to make a concerted effort to be sure your current pet(s) know you will still care for them. Set a specific time in your schedule when you can show your current dog(s) how much you love him (them), and make sure you don't stray from that schedule after the puppy arrives.

When you bring the puppy home, plan to have at least one adult present for each dog you have in your home. If you have a cat in the home, the introduction will need to be slow and methodical. If you bring home an adult Leonberger, you will need to be careful and keep the dog and cat separated when you aren't around to monitor them. Over time, it is likely they will learn to be fine with each other.

Having a schedule in place for your other dogs will make it easier to follow the plan with the puppy. Once he has arrived, your puppy is going to eat, sleep, and spend most of the day and night in his assigned space. This means your puppy's space cannot block your current canine's favorite furniture, bed, or anywhere he rests during the day. None of your current dog's "stuff" should be in the puppy's area either; this includes toys. You don't want your older dog to feel as if the puppy is taking over his territory. Make sure your children also understand to never put your current dog's things in the puppy's area!

Your dog and your puppy will need to be kept apart at the beginning (even if they seem friendly) until your puppy has received his vaccinations. Puppies are more susceptible to illness during these early days, so wait until the puppy is protected from possible diseases before the dogs spend time together. Leaving the puppy in his puppy space will keep them separated during this critical time.

Helping Your Dog Prepare – Extra at Home Playdates

The following explains strategies that will help prepare your current pooch for the arrival of your puppy:

- Consider the personality of your dog to predict what might happen when the puppy arrives. If your current dog loves other dogs, this will probably hold true when the puppy shows up. If your current dog is territorial, you will need to be cautious when introducing the two dogs, at

Photo Courtesy
of Jan Meendering

least until the Leonberger has become part of the pack. Excitable dogs need special attention to keep them from getting agitated when a new dog comes home. You don't want your current dog to be so excited that he makes the Leonberger feel threatened.

- Consider the times when unfamiliar dogs have been in your home. How did your current dog react to these other furry visitors? If your canine becomes territorial, be cautious when introducing your new pup. If you have never invited another dog into your home, organize a playdate with other dogs before your Leonberger puppy arrives. You need to know how your current furry babies will react to new dogs in the house so that you can properly prepare. Meeting a dog at home is quite different from encountering one outside the home.

- Think about your established dog's interactions with other dogs for as long as you have known him. Has your dog shown protective or possessive behavior, either with you or others? Food is one of the reasons dogs will display aggression because they don't want anyone eating what is theirs. Some dogs can be protective of people and toys too.

- If you know someone who owns a Leonberger, organize a playdate so that your current dog becomes aware of the temperament of a Leonberger.

These same rules apply, no matter how many dogs you have. Think about their individual personalities as well as how they interact together. Similar to humans, you may find when your dogs are together, they act differently. This is something you will need to keep in mind as you plan their first introduction. (Details of how to introduce your current dog(s) and your new puppy—plus how to juggle the two new personalities—are included in Chapter 9.)

CHAPTER 6

Preparing Your Home and Schedule

The amount of time you need to spend preparing your home for a puppy versus an adult is about the same, but what you have to do is going to be very different. With a puppy, you are essentially going to need to childproof your home for toddlers. With an adult, you are going to need to home-proof it for a larger child, more with gates to keep your dog contained to certain areas as you figure out just how your dog will interact with the surroundings. Doors

Photo Courtesy of MacKenzie Jones

HELPFUL TIP
A Crate for All Stages

Leonberger puppies typically weigh between 11 and 14 pounds at three months old, only a fraction of their full size. Adult Leonbergers weigh from 90 to 160 pounds, with females weighing less than their male counterparts at the lower end of this range. This considerable size discrepancy means that your puppy will soon outgrow its "puppy-sized" crate. But what if you don't want to continue buying crates for your dog? Crates with a moveable divider are a perfect choice! Purchase a crate that will fit your Leonberger's estimated full size and use the partition to create a smaller space within your crate for the puppy. Make sure your puppy has enough room to stand up and turn around comfortably as it grows. Making your puppy's space too big can delay house-training.

may be enough, but you'll want gates and a dedicated area for both puppies and adults.

When it comes to puppies, it really is almost exactly like child-proofing your home prior to the arrival of a baby or toddler. Protecting your Leonberger is the priority, and as hard as it can be to believe, they are small for at least a few months. For adult dogs, you need to make sure that they aren't able to get out of the yard or make their way into rooms that are potentially dangerous for them. Even after you've completed the initial preparations, a weekly review leading up to your Leonberger's arrival is necessary to make sure you don't miss anything and that everything is in place. You will need to check higher areas for an adult Leonberger than for smaller dogs, especially when it comes to cords, etc. Your new family member should have a safe space that includes all of the essentials. This will help to make your dog more comfortable and make the initial arrival a great experience for everyone.

As an intelligent breed, the Leonberger has to know that you are the leader to follow and listen to, so you will need to earn your new family member's respect, which is easier with a puppy than it is with an adult (though it is easier to make exceptions for a puppy over an adult, which you should not do). This is why it is absolutely essential to ensure that you are firm and consistent when you are training and working with your Leonberger. When he understands that you mean what you say, that will go a long way to letting him know why he should listen to you.

Photo Courtesy
of Maria Wallace

Creating a Safe Space for Your Adult Dog or Puppy

Your new dog will need a dedicated space that includes a crate, food and water bowls, pee pads, and toys. All of these things should be in the area where the puppy will stay when you are not able to give him attention. The puppy's space should be gated so that your Leonberger cannot get out and young children (or dogs) cannot get in. It should be a safe space where the puppy can see you going about your usual business and feel comfortable.

An adult Leonberger will need a similar setup as a puppy, with all of the same items, but you can give the adult dog a bigger area. Pee pads may be necessary while the adult dog adjusts to the new environment, even if the dog is already house-trained.

Crates

> They get HOT so easily. They will not be happy in a crate with a fluffy pad. Leo puppies are happiest when sleeping on a cool floor. It's good to give them a cozy option, but most likely, they will go for the cool option! I use a puppy pen instead of a crate for my pups.
>
> ELLIE ADAMS
> *Rocky Ford Leonbergers*

Crate training (discussed in detail in Chapter 7) is much more likely to be difficult if you have a crate that is too big, too small, or too uncomfortable for your dog to feel like it is a safe place to be in. To make training easier, be sure the crate and bedding are set up and ready before your dog arrives. A small, cozy space will help your dog feel comfortable while also dissuading him from using it as a restroom since he won't be able to get away from any mess he makes.

Never treat the crate like it is a prison for your puppy or adult dog. It's meant to be a safe haven after overstimulation or when it's time to sleep. Ensure your dog never associates the crate with punishment or negative emotions. You can also get your puppy a carrying crate in the early days to make trips to the vet easier. Both puppies and adults are going to spend a good bit of time in the crate in those early days, though adults will be able to roam your home a lot faster than a puppy. At least, if the adult is already house-trained, it will be a much faster process to get away from the crate.

Photo Courtesy of Tom Mueller

Puppy-Proof/Dog-Proof the House

> **"**
>
> *I encourage owners to block off any stairs, as puppies shouldn't use large flights of stairs until fully grown. Slippery floors should have area rugs to assist with traction. A step or ramp may be needed to assist puppies into vehicles. Leo puppies love to play in their water, so a non-tipping water bowl and a bath mat under it are highly advisable! Always remember that while puppy antics might be cute and adorable, those same antics might not be acceptable in a 140-pound dog, so train your dog while its young!*
>
> ERIN ANDERSEN
> *High Hopes Newfoundlands and Leonbergers*
>
> **"**

The most dangerous rooms and items in your home will be as dangerous to your puppy as if he were a little baby. The biggest difference is your Leonberger is going to become mobile much faster than a child. He will get into dangerous situations immediately if you don't eliminate all the hazards before his arrival. Be aware that puppies will try to eat virtually anything! Nothing is safe—not even your furniture—and they will also gnaw on wood and metal or clothing. Anything within reach is considered fair game! This is true for adult dogs too, but clearly, their reach will be a lot higher off the ground, including in your kitchen.

Keep this in mind as you go about puppy-proofing your home. You will need to look for all of these dangers and make sure they are removed before your Leonberger arrives, whether the dog is a puppy or an adult.

Plant Dangers

You will need to be mindful of the plants in and around your home that could be hazardous to your dog. The following are various plants that should not be within your dog's reach. Remember to check both inside and outside your home.

Mildly Toxic	Mildly to Moderately Toxic	Moderately Toxic	Moderately to Highly Toxic	Highly Toxic
Asparagus Fern	Aloe	Alocasia	Cactus	Brunfelsia
Begonia	Amaryllis	Arrowhead	Kalanchoe	Desert Rose
Ficus Benjamina	Calla Lily	Dieffenbachia		Flame Lily
Flamingo Flower	Cyclamen	Dracaena Fragrans		Kaffir Lily
Gardenia	Dracaena	English Ivy		Oleander
Geranium	Philodendron	Eucalyptus		Sago Palm
Golden Pothos		Peyote		Bird of Paradise (Strelitzia)
Jade Plant				
Schefflera				
Ti Plant				

Indoor Hazards and Fixes

> **"**
>
> *Leos seem to enjoy spreading their drinking water everywhere, so maybe find a spot for the water bowl that is out of the way of traffic.*
>
> PEGGY ATCHLEY
> *Great Northern Leonbergers*
>
> **"**

A Leonberger will be an avid explorer, wanting to get into everything if given the opportunity. Get on your hands and knees to view each room from your Leonberger's perspective prior to the dog's arrival.

Hazards	Fixes	Time Estimate
KITCHEN		
Poisons	Keep in secure, childproof cabinets or on high shelves.	30 min.
Trash Cans	Use a lockable trash can or keep it in a secure location.	10 min.
Appliances	Make sure all cords are out of reach.	15 min.
Human Food	Keep out of reach.	Constant (Start making it a habit!)
FLOORS		
Slippery Surfaces	Put down rugs or special mats designed to stick to the floor.	30 min. – 1 hour
Training Area	Train your Leonberger on nonslip surfaces.	Constant
BATHROOMS		
Toilet Brush	Either have one that locks into the container or keep the brush out of reach.	5 min.
Poisons	Keep in secure, childproof cabinets or on high shelves.	15–30 min.
Toilets	Keep lids closed. Do not use automatic toilet-cleaning chemicals.	Constant (Start making it a habit!)
Cabinets	Keep locked with childproof locks.	15–30 min.
LAUNDRY ROOM		
Clothing	Store clean and dirty clothes off the floor and out of reach.	15–30 min.
Poisons (bleach, pods/detergent, dryer sheets, and misc. poisons)	Keep in secure, childproof cabinets or on high shelves.	15 min.
AROUND THE HOME		
Plants	Keep off the floor.	45 min. – 1 hour
Trash Cans	Have a lockable trash can or keep it in a secure location.	10–30 min.

Hazards	Fixes	Time Estimate
Electrical Cords/ Window Blind Cords	Hide cords or make sure they are out of reach; pay particular attention to entertainment and computer areas.	1–1.5 hours
Poisons	Check to make sure there aren't any in reach (WD40, window/screen cleaner, carpet cleaner, air fresheners); move all poisons to a central, locked location.	1 hour
Windows	Be sure cords are out of reach in all rooms.	1–2 hours
Fireplaces	Store cleaning supplies and tools where the puppy can't get into them. Cover the fireplace opening with something the puppy can't knock over.	10 min.
Stairs	Cordon off so that your puppy can't go up or down the stairs; make sure to test all puppy gates for safety.	10–15 min.
Coffee Tables/ End Tables/ Nightstands	Clear of dangerous objects (e.g., scissors, sewing equipment, pens, and pencils) and all valuables.	30–45 min.

If you have a cat, keep the litter box off the floor. It needs to be somewhere that your cat can easily get to it, but your Leonberger cannot. Since this involves training your cat, it's something you should do well in advance of the dog's arrival. You don't want your cat to undergo too many significant changes all at once. The new canine in the house will be enough of a disruption! If your cat associates the change with your Leonberger, you may find the feline refusing to use the litter box.

To get the litter box out of your dog's reach, you'll need to put it up high and preferably somewhere that doesn't have a chair that your dog can use to get to it. Clever pups can figure out how to get to places where you think they wouldn't be able to go.

Finally, in case of problems, be sure your vet's number is posted on the fridge and in at least one other room in the house. Even if the number is programmed into your phone, family members or dog sitters will still need to know who to call.

Outdoor Hazards and Fixes

The area outside your home also needs dog-proofing. As with the inside, you will need to check your outdoor preparations by getting down low and inspecting all areas from a puppy's perspective. Remember to also post the vet's number in one of the sheltered outdoor areas in case of an emergency.

Hazards	Fixes	Time Estimate
GARAGE		
Poisons	Keep in secure, childproof cabinets or on high shelves (e.g., car chemicals, cleaning supplies, paint, lawn care) – this includes fertilizer.	1 hour
Trash Bins	Keep them in a secure location.	5 min.
Tools (e.g., lawn, car, hardware, power tools)	Make sure all cords are kept out of reach and never hang over the side of surfaces.	30 min. - 1 hour
Equipment (e.g., sports, fishing)	Keep out of reach, and never allow them to hang over the side of surfaces.	Constant (Start making it a habit!)
Sharp Implements	Keep out of reach, and never allow them to hang over the side of surfaces.	30 min.
Bikes	Store off the ground or in a place the Leonberger cannot get to (to keep the pup from biting the tires).	20 min.
FENCING (CAN BE DONE CONCURRENTLY)		
Breaks	Fix any breaks in the fencing. You need to make sure your Leonberger can't easily get out of your yard.	30 min. - 1 hour
Gaps	Fill in any gaps so your Leonberger doesn't escape.	30 min. - 1 hour
Holes/Dips at Base	Fill in any area that can be easily crawled under.	1–2 hours
YARD		
Poisons	Don't leave any poisons in the yard.	1–2 hours
Plants	Verify that low plants aren't poisonous; fence off anything that is (such as grapevines).	45 min. - 1 hour

If you have a pool, make sure it is secure so that your dog cannot get into it without your help. Covers may not always be enough (especially for intelligent breeds that may want to swim on their own terms), so make sure to have fencing or some other kind of deterrent to keep your Leonberger safe. Even if your dog loves swimming, make sure you are always around when your dog is in the pool. Leonbergers tend to love swimming, but it's best not to let them jump in the water without supervision.

Never leave your Leonberger alone in the garage, even when the dog is an adult. Your puppy may be in the garage when you take car trips, which is why it is important to puppy-proof this area. An adult can get up to even more trouble, which is pretty much inevitable when he gets bored.

Make room in your schedule for monthly inspections because Leonbergers may dig out of boredom or could damage a fence as a form of entertainment. This is also why you can never leave your Leonberger alone outside. Always attend to your dog when he goes out to the bathroom or to play because when he is bored, he will very likely start to create ways out of the yard. You don't want to put him out to use the bathroom only to find he has escaped in the five minutes you left him outside alone.

Choosing Your Veterinarian

You should choose a vet before you bring your dog home because scheduling a veterinary appointment may take a while. Unfortunately, you may not find a vet who has some experience with the breed. Try to find a vet that at least has some experience with bigger work dogs.

Every dog, regardless of age, should see a vet within the first forty-eight hours of its arrival home. The point is to establish your dog's baseline health. This may also be a requirement included in the contract with the breeder. Twenty-four hours is strongly recommended to make sure your dog is healthy, but this may not always be possible, which is why many places say to have it done within 48 hours. If there is a vet near you who specializes in or has worked with Leonbergers before, that will be best for your pup.

The following are some things to consider when looking for a vet:

- What is the vet's level of familiarity with Leonbergers or similar large dogs, like Saint Bernards and Newfoundlands?

  It is almost guaranteed that vets in your area will not have experience with the breed, but experience with bigger work dogs is usually helpful with learning how to treat a Leonberger.

- How far from your home is the vet?

You don't want the vet to be more than 30 minutes away in case of an emergency.

Photo Courtesy of Storme Gabriel

- Is the vet available for emergencies after hours, or can they recommend a vet in case of an emergency?
- Is the vet part of a local veterinary hospital, or does the vet refer patients to a local pet hospital?
- Is the vet one of several partners, or do they work alone? If the vet belongs to a partnership, can your dog see the same vet for all office visits?
- How are appointments booked?
- Can other services be performed at the clinic, such as grooming and boarding?
- Is the vet accredited?
- What is the price for the initial visit? What are the costs for routine visits that might include such things as shots?
- What tests and checks are performed during the initial visit?
- Can you visit the vet you are considering before you bring your dog home?

    If so, inspect the office environment and ask if you can speak to the vet. The vet should be willing to put you at ease and answer your questions. Even though a vet's time is valuable, they should take a few minutes to help you feel confident about your decision to trust them with your new dog's health.

CHAPTER 7
Bringing Your Leonberger Home

> "
>
> *Leonbergers grow fast. You have to puppy-proof areas that a normal puppy would not be able to reach (coffee tables, kitchen tables, dressers). You also have to be sure that you take puppy classes and obedience classes seriously because before you know it, you will have a 100-pound puppy with a puppy brain, and you will have to have laid good groundwork for manners and not jumping or pulling.*
>
> SUE HERMAN
> *Water's Edge Leonbergers*
>
> "

Seeing your Leonberger coming into your home that first time is a memorable moment. Your dog is almost certain to make you laugh as you try to keep him from getting into trouble. His curiosity and interest will give you a completely different perspective of your world. It will almost certainly be a time of excitement and chaos. Between acclimating your dog to a new home and getting everyone on the same page (something that becomes increasingly difficult the more people and pets you have), you will definitely have your work cut out for you. Take the time to enjoy your newest family member's arrival, but also be aware of how overwhelming the experience can be for your dog.

This chapter covers how to introduce your new Leonberger to your home. If you already have a dog, refer to Chapter 8 because you will need to introduce the animals outside of the home before your pup makes his grand entrance. Once you understand how to introduce dogs to each other, come back to this chapter to learn how to introduce your new family member to your home and any family members who weren't able to make the initial meet and greet.

If you don't have dogs, read ahead to see what to expect and how to make the experience more enjoyable for your Leonberger.

Photo Courtesy
of Rachel Brastock

Final Preparations and Planning

If you are bringing home a puppy, there are good odds that there will be a lot of anxiety and nervousness. Adult dogs are less likely to feel this way unless they were at their previous home long enough to get comfortable (this is usually not the case at shelters or similar rescues), but they will still feel some level of anxiety and be wary in their new surroundings. You can try to prepare to minimize the negative emotions, starting with taking time off from work during the first 24 to 48 hours; the best-case scenario would have you at home for the first week or two. The more time you dedicate to helping your new friend become accustomed to his surroundings, the better.

Ensure You Have Food and Other Supplies on Hand

The day before your Leonberger arrives, review the list in Chapter 5 and do a quick check to ensure you have everything you need. Take a few moments to consider if there is anything you are missing. This will keep you from having to rush out for additional supplies after the arrival of your new family member.

Design a Tentative Puppy Schedule

> **"**
>
> *It's good to start out with a routine (just like human babies, puppies do best with some predictability), so have a designated time for eating, playing, resting, walking, snuggling throughout the day, and try to keep this schedule pretty predictable for the first few weeks!*
>
> ELLIE ADAMS
> *Rocky Ford Leonbergers*
>
> **"**

Prepare a tentative schedule to help you get started over the course of the first week. Your days are about to get remarkably busy, so you need somewhere to begin before your puppy arrives. As you settle more into a routine, you can update the schedule so it isn't set in stone. Consider it more of a guideline so that you don't forget important tasks, especially taking your dog out for regular restroom breaks.

The following are three key areas to establish before your puppy arrives:

- Feeding
- Training (including house-training)
- Playing.

When you bring home a puppy, you may be expecting a ball of high energy. However, puppies of any breed (no matter how active they will be later) sleep between 18 and 20 hours per day. Having a predictable sleep schedule will help your puppy grow up to be healthier. Plan eating times, bathroom breaks, and playtime around your puppy's sleep schedule.

In the beginning, you won't need to worry about making sure that your puppy is tired out by the end of the day. His stamina will build fairly quickly, though; by the end of the first year, your pup will be a lot more active! As your pup starts to sleep less and play more, he will need 30 to 60 minutes of daily physical activity. In the early days, your puppy's schedule will revolve around sleeping and eating, with some walking and socialization. Waking hours will include training and play.

Photo Courtesy of Marita McCahill

Every puppy is different, even within a single breed, so adjust the schedule based on the changes you see with your own puppy.

Do a Quick Final Puppy-Readiness Inspection Before the Puppy Arrives

No matter how busy you are or how carefully you follow the puppy-proofing checklist, the day before your puppy arrives, be sure to set aside an hour or two to double-check that everything is in place.

Initial Meeting

Review the rules in Chapter 5 with all family members the day of the dog's arrival and before the pup actually arrives. Place heavy emphasis on how to handle the Leonberger, particularly the part about not picking up your newest family member. The puppy is already going to be in a state of shock, so don't compound that by literally taking the world out from under your Leonberger's feet.

Keep in mind that Leonbergers tend to be wary of strangers. All of this will need to be kept in mind so that the family is careful about the first interaction. Everyone needs to be aware to let the dog start interactions; people should not be screaming, squealing, or being otherwise very noisy, as this can be a source of anxiety for the Leonberger. People should also not crowd around the puppy.

Determine who is going to be responsible for the primary puppy care and for primary training. To teach younger children responsibility, a parent can pair with a child to manage the puppy's care. The child can be responsible for feeding the puppy and keeping the water bowl filled. Of course, a parent should oversee these tasks.

HELPFUL TIP
Car Safety

The safest place in the car for your dog, especially a puppy, is secured in a crate. Some crates are specifically designed for cars and made with padding to protect your dog from an impact. Your Leonberger puppy doesn't require a full-size crate, but the crate should be large enough for your dog to stand up and turn around comfortably. Dog seat belts are another safe option, but be sure to steer clear of the airbags in the front seats. The most dangerous places for your Leonberger pup are in the driver's lap and the vehicle's passenger seat.

Picking up Your Puppy or Dog and the Ride Home

> **"**
>
> *Be patient! Remember, this is a new adventure for your puppy and the first time away from his/her siblings. I highly recommend crate training. Hopefully, your breeder will have sent a toy scented by mum and littermates. That can be helpful while transitioning. I typically encourage new puppy parents to bring a bed or blanket that they will be using to the puppy pickup and scent that as well.*
>
> ERIN ANDERSEN
> *High Hopes Newfoundlands and Leonbergers*
> **"**

A good bit of planning and preparation goes into picking up your puppy, especially if you are going to the breeder's home. If possible, do this on a weekend or during a holiday season. This will allow you unrushed quality time at home with your new puppy.

As tempting as it is to cuddle the puppy in your lap, it is safer and more comfortable for the puppy if you use a crate for the ride home; two adults should also be present for the ride. This is the time to start teaching your puppy that car trips are enjoyable. This means making sure that the crate is securely anchored; you don't want the crate to slide around while the puppy is helplessly sitting inside.

- The crate should be anchored in the car for safety and should include a cushion. If you have a long trip, bring food and water for the puppy and plan to stop at different intervals. Do not put food and water in the crate; sloshing water can scare your puppy. You can cover the bottom of the crate with a towel or pee pad in case of accidents.

- Call the breeder before you start the trip to make sure everything is still on schedule.

- Arrange for the mother dog to leave her scent on a blanket to help make the puppy's transition more comfortable.

- Make sure the second adult will be on time so that the two of you can head to the pick-up destination.

- If you have other dogs, make sure all of the adults involved in the introduction process know what to do. They should know the time and place for that first neutral territory meeting.

If you do not have other dogs, you can pick up your puppy and head straight home. If you have a trip that lasts more than a couple of hours, stop periodically so your puppy can stretch, exercise, drink, and use the bathroom. Keep your puppy away from other dogs until he has gotten all of his shots; you don't want him to be exposed to a dog that is carrying a disease that your puppy is not fully protected against.

At no point should your puppy be left alone in the car. If you have to use the restroom, either go before leaving the breeder's place, or if you have a long drive ahead of you, have at least one adult remain with the puppy during each stop.

If the puppy has never ridden in a car before, someone should give the puppy attention while the other person drives. The puppy should still be in the crate, but someone can still provide comfort. The puppy will definitely be scared without his mom, siblings, or familiar people to console him. Having someone talk to the puppy will make it less of an ordeal for the little one.

When you arrive home, immediately take the puppy outside to use the bathroom. Even if he had an accident in his crate, this is the time to start training your new family member on where to use the bathroom.

The First Vet Visit and What to Expect

The first vet visit will establish a baseline for the puppy's health. This will also allow the vet to track your puppy's progress and monitor his health as he grows. In addition to providing a chance to ask questions and get advice, this initial assessment will give you more information about your puppy. It also creates an important rapport between your Leonberger and the vet.

During the first veterinary visit, your pup won't know what to expect. Try to ease his anxiety; you want this first appointment to set a positive tone for all future visits. This will likely be trickier with an adult dog than with a puppy, so be prepared to soothe any nervousness.

The following is a list of several things that must be completed before the day of the appointment:

- Find out how early you need to arrive to complete the paperwork for the new patient.
- Find out if you should bring a stool sample for that first visit. If so, collect it the morning of the visit and make sure to take it with you.

Photo Courtesy
of Lili Costagliola

- Bring the paperwork provided by the breeder or rescue organization for the vet to add to your dog's records.

Upon your arrival, your Leonberger may want to meet the other pups and people in the office and will probably loudly announce your arrival. Although you will need to be mindful, this is an opportunity to socialize the puppy and to create a positive experience with the vet. Before letting your puppy meet other animals, always ask the owner for permission and wait for approval. Most pets at the vet's office are likely to not be feeling well, which means they may not be very affable. You don't want a grumpy, older dog or a sick animal to nip or scare your puppy. Negative social experiences are situations your puppy will remember; they could make future visits to the vet something to dread. Nor do you want your puppy to be exposed to potential illnesses before he has had all of his shots.

Every vet is different, so you should call your vet ahead of your first visit to get an idea of everything that will be done. Odds are, you will need to bring documentation about your dog, so this can also serve as a reminder to get your paperwork together and ready to go with you and your newest family member when you go to the vet the first time.

Young puppies will need a series of shots. The vet may also request that you bring your dog's latest poop to check it for parasites. Chapter 16 provides more details on what to expect if parasites are detected in your dog's bowel movement.

Be prepared for the vet to ask about your dog's history, even though you just brought the Leonberger home with you.

During the first visit, the vet will conduct an initial assessment of your Leonberger. One of the most important things the vet will do is weigh your dog. This is something you are going to have to monitor for your dog's entire life, as you will want to ensure that your Leonberger remains at a healthy weight. Keep a record of his weight so you can see how quickly your puppy is growing and to make sure you aren't overfeeding him or are feeding him enough. Ask your vet what is considered a healthy weight for every growth stage and record that as well.

The vet will set a date for the next group of shots, which will likely happen not too long after the initial visit. After your Leonberger receives his vaccinations (detailed in Chapter 16), prepare for a couple of days of your puppy feeling under the weather.

The following are other checks the vet may make during that initial visit.

- Most vets will listen to your dog's heart and lungs to make sure there aren't any obvious problems.
- They will take your pup's temperature, so be prepared to help by calming your dog, as he's probably not going to be happy with this activity.
- Vets usually check a dog's ears, eyes, nose, paws, skin/coat, and genitals.
- They will do a longer check on the mouth and teeth to look for potential problems.
- They will do an initial check on the abdomen and lymph nodes.

If the vet does find a problem and recommends medication, take the time to ask questions and make sure you know what to do before you leave the office.

Crate and Other Preliminary Training

Contrary to what some people think, crates are a safe space for dogs. Crate training will also prepare your dog for occasions when you may have to board him, and he will be put in a crate if you ever travel on a plane.

Puppies younger than six months should not be left in a crate for hours at a time. Your Leonberger will not be able to hold his bladder for very long, so you must make sure he has a way to get out and to go to the bathroom. If you adopt an adult Leonberger that is not house-trained, you will need to follow the same rules. If you aren't sure about whether or not the dog is house-trained, it is best to treat the adult as a puppy until you are certain that your newest family member won't use the house as a bathroom.

Make sure the crate door is set so that it doesn't close on your dog during his initial sniff of the crate. You do not want your Leonberger to be scared by the door as it is closing behind him; this could make him fearful of the crate in the future.

The following are some suggestions:

- Use a positive, cheerful voice as you let your Leonberger sniff the crate for the first time. The first experience in the crate should be associated with excitement and positive emotions. Be sure your dog understands the crate is a good place. If you have a blanket from the puppy's mother, put it in the crate to help provide an extra sense of comfort.

- Drop a couple of treats into the crate if your canine seems reluctant to enter. Do NOT force your dog into the crate. If your dog refuses to go all the way inside the crate, that is perfectly fine. It has to be the dog's decision to enter, so it doesn't become a negative experience.

- For a week or two, feed your dog while he is in the crate. Besides keeping the food away from any other pets, this will create positive associations between your Leonberger and the crate.

  - If your dog appears comfortable with the crate, put the food all the way at the back.

  - If not, place the food bowl in the front, then move it further back in the crate over time.

Photo Courtesy of Barbara Zwierzynska

- Start closing the door once your dog appears to be eating comfortably in the crate. When the food is gone, open the crate door immediately.

- Leave the door closed for longer periods of time after your dog has finished eating. If your pup begins to whine, you know you have left your Leonberger in the crate for too long.

- Crate your dog for longer periods of time once the dog

shows no signs of discomfort while in the crate when eating. Train your Leonberger to go into the crate by simply saying, "Crate" or "Bed." Then, praise your dog to let him know that he has done an excellent job.

Repeat these steps for several weeks until your dog seems comfortable in the crate. The regular repetition several times a day teaches your dog that the crate is not a punishment and everything is all right. Initially, you should do this while you are still at home or when you go out to get the mail. When you leave the room, and your puppy lasts half an hour without whining, you can leave the dog alone for longer periods of time. However, keep this alone time to no more than an hour in the beginning.

During the first few weeks, you should also begin to house-train your Leonberger. Basic behavioral training is also vital from the start. However, wait until your Leonberger has all of his vaccinations before taking your new puppy to structured training classes. Knowledgeable trainers will not accept puppies in their classes until a dog's first full round of shots is complete.

Chapters 10 and 11 provide a closer look at how to train your dog.

First-Night Frights

> *All puppies are scared and lonely for their littermates and mothers the first few days. Send a box of towels or blankets to the breeder and ask to have those placed in the puppy box so they will be covered with the smells of your Leo's siblings and mom, which will help to ease the transition. Do not be afraid to spend extra time sleeping and snuggling with your puppy the first few nights to help your Leo through the transition. This will improve your bond and also help to decrease the pup's anxiety and loneliness.*
>
> SUE HERMAN
> *Water's Edge Leonbergers*

That first night is going to be terrifying for your little Leonberger puppy! As understandable as this may be, there is only so much comfort you can give your new family member. The more you respond to his cries and whimpering, the more he will learn negative behavior provides the desired results. You need to prepare for a balancing act—one that reassures the Leonberger that he is safe while keeping him from associating crying with receiving attention from you.

Create a sleeping area for your puppy near where you sleep. The area should have the puppy's bed tucked safely into his crate. This will offer him a safe place to hide and a place where he will feel more comfortable in this strange new home. The entire area should be blocked off to be sure no one can get in (and the puppy can't get out) during the night. This sleeping area should also be close to where people sleep so that the puppy doesn't feel abandoned. If you were able to get a blanket or pillow that smells like the dog's mother, make sure that this is in your puppy's space. Consider adding a little white noise (like an old-fashioned alarm clock) to cover unfamiliar sounds that could scare your new pet.

Your puppy will make noises over the course of the night. Don't move the puppy away, even if the whimpering keeps you awake. Being moved away from people will only scare him more, reinforcing the feeling of anxiety. When your puppy whines during the night, he is not whimpering because he's been in the crate too long. He's scared or wants someone to be with him—he's probably never been alone at night before coming to live with you. Spare yourself trouble later on by teaching the puppy that whimpering will not get him out of the crate. Over time, being close to you at night will be enough to reassure your puppy that everything will be fine.

In the beginning, puppies will need to go to the bathroom every two to three hours. This means you will also need to get up during the night! Make sure your puppy understands he must always go to the bathroom outside before bedtime or on the pee pad. If you ignore this rule, you will have a tough time training your dog to only relieve himself outside and not in the house.

If you choose to let your dog on the bed, wait until he is house-trained. Otherwise, you might have to replace your mattress within a short time. It is best to simply keep your Leonberger off the furniture so that he doesn't get hurt and your furniture doesn't get ruined!

CHAPTER 8

Introducing Your Leonberger to Your Other Dogs

Depending on the age of the dog, the initial introductions could be challenging. Leonberger puppies tend to be easier to introduce than adult dogs, but you will want to take the same steps to introduce your new dog, no matter how old both animals are. Nearly all dogs are hesitant initially when they meet another dog in a completely new environment. If you have other dogs, it is a chance to begin socializing your new Leonberger (Chapter 12). Leonbergers aren't as friendly with other dogs as they are with their family, but when properly socialized, they can be great friends (and even guardians) of their other canine companions.

HISTORICAL FACT
Nearly Vanished

The Leonberger breed was nearly wiped out in World War I, but thanks to Karl Stadelmann and Otto Josenhans, the breed survives today. After the war sharply diminished the population of these dogs, Stadelmann and Josenhans rounded up 25 dogs who best represented their vision for the breed and formed a breeding cooperative. Four years later, 350 Leonbergers had been bred, effectively rescuing the breed from extinction.

It is actually best if you have at least one other dog so that your Leonberger isn't home alone while you are out shopping or at work. If you already have a socialized adult dog, your current dog can also help teach your new Leonberger the rules, and he could even become a mentor to your puppy. If you adopt a puppy, he may imitate your current dog's obedience when you give directions, something that could be really helpful with a potentially stubborn breed. However, this works both ways. If your current dog displays negative behavior,

Photo Courtesy of Kelly Klocker

you should try to correct these habits before your puppy arrives. You don't want your Leonberger pup learning bad habits.

As tempting as it may be, it is best not to bring two puppies into the home at the same time, especially from the same litter. They are much more likely to have a stronger bond with each other than with you or your family. Taking on one puppy at a time and having an adult to help you with that puppy is much more likely to have the best results.

Introducing Your New Puppy to Your Other Pets

It doesn't matter what breed your new dog is—introducing him to your current dogs is always something that should be planned and monitored. Even if you feel you know your current dogs, bringing a new dog into the mix can be a challenge. This section details the best way to introduce a puppy to your dogs in an environment that should remove a lot of the potential issues that may make dogs warier.

Introduce all new dogs to your current dog or dogs, regardless of age, in a neutral place away from your home. Even if you have never had problems with your current dog, you are about to change his world. When introducing your dog to the new puppy, select a park or other public area so your current dog will not feel territorial. This gives both animals the opportunity to meet and become familiar with each other on neutral ground.

When introducing the two dogs, make sure you have at least one other adult with you so that there's one person for each canine. All dogs should be leashed so that you can quickly and easily move them apart if the introduction does not go well. If you have more than two dogs, then you should have one adult per dog. This will make it easier to keep all of the dogs under control. Even the best dogs can get excited about meeting a puppy. One of the people who needs to be at this meeting is the person who is in charge of the pets in your home. This helps establish the pack hierarchy.

Don't hold your puppy in your arms when the dogs meet. While you may want to protect the puppy, holding him has the opposite effect. Instead, your puppy will feel trapped, but if the puppy is on the ground, he can run if he feels scared. Stand near the puppy with your feet a little bit apart, so the dog can hide behind your legs if he decides he needs to escape.

All dogs should have a few minutes to sniff each other, making sure there is always some slack on each leash. Feeling like they can move more freely helps dogs to relax, and they won't feel like you are trying to restrain them or force them into something. Your dog will either want to play, or he might simply ignore the puppy. You need to let your dog dictate what happens next. If the dogs want to play, be careful your current dog doesn't accidentally hurt the puppy, and if your dog ends up ignoring the puppy after an initial sniff, that is fine too. If your dog is clearly unhappy, keep all of the dogs apart until everyone is comfortable with the meeting. Don't force the situation.

This introduction could take a while, depending on each individual dog's personality. The friendlier and more accepting your current dog is, the easier it will be to incorporate your new puppy into the home. For some dogs, a week is enough time to start feeling comfortable together. For other dogs, it could take a couple of months before they are fully accepting of a new puppy. Since this is a completely new dynamic for your dog, he may be angry with you for bringing this new bundle of energy into his life.

The older your current dog is, the more likely it is that a puppy will be an unwelcome addition. Older dogs can get cranky around a puppy that doesn't know when enough is enough! The goal is to make your puppy feel welcome and safe and to let your older dog know that your love for him is as strong as ever.

Once your new family member and the rest of the canine pack become acquainted and comfortable, you can head home. When you arrive, take the dogs into the yard and remove the leashes. Again, you will need one adult per dog, including the puppy. If the dogs are all right or are indifferent to the puppy, you can let your current dog inside. Then, re-leash the puppy, keeping him on the leash as you go inside. This is also a good time to take the puppy to the bathroom before going in so that he knows where to go.

Put the puppy in the puppy area when the introductions are complete. Remember to make sure your current dog cannot get into this area and your puppy cannot get out.

Introducing an Adult Dog to Other Pets

Always approach the introduction (and first few weeks together) with caution. The new adult Leonberger will need his own things from the very beginning—Leonbergers can be territorial if not properly trained. When you aren't around, your dog should be kept in a separate area so there won't be any fighting among the dogs. One thing to note is that some experts recommend that you do not have two adult Leonbergers of the same sex together, as they may not get along.

Plan for this introduction to take at least an hour. Since the dogs are both adults, they will need to move and become acquainted at their own pace.

When introducing your current dog(s) to your new dog, follow the same steps as you would with a puppy:

- Begin in neutral territory.
- Ask one adult to be present for each adult canine during the introduction.
- Introduce one dog at a time. Don't let several dogs meet your new Leonberger all at once.

Bring treats to the meeting of two adult dogs—unlike with puppies. The animals will respond to the treats, and if the atmosphere becomes tense, the treats will create a distraction.

During the introduction, watch the Leonberger and your dog(s) to see if any of them raise their hackles. This is one of the first obvious signs that a dog is uncomfortable. If the Leonberger's hackles are up, back off the introductions for a little bit. Do this by calling your current dog back first. This is also when you should start waving treats around! Avoid pulling on the leashes to separate the dogs. You don't want to add physical tension to the situation because that could trigger a fight. Treats will work for all dogs, and calling their names should help get things under control.

If any of the dogs are showing their teeth or growling, call your dog back and give them a chance to settle down. Use treats and a calming voice to get them to relax. You want all the dogs to feel comfortable during the first meeting, so don't force the friendship. If they seem uncomfortable or wary at first, let them move at their own pace.

Older Dogs and Your Leonberger

If your current dog is older, keep in mind puppies are energetic, and they want to engage older dogs in play. This can be very trying for your older canine, so make sure your older dog doesn't get too tired of the puppy's antics. A tired older dog could snap and nip at your puppy in hopes of getting a little rest. You don't want your puppy to begin snapping at other dogs too. Watch for signs your older dog is ready for some alone time, some time with you, or simply a break from the puppy. Given how energetic and noisy Leonbergers can be, you want to ensure that your older dog has a place to hide away so that he can relax.

You should always make sure your older dog has safe places to be alone. This is essential for those times he just doesn't feel up to being around a spry, young puppy! By keeping your puppy and your older dog separated, you can prevent the need for constant scolding. Plus, the puppy will not become wary of older dogs.

Even if you rescue an adult Leonberger, he might still be too energetic for your older dog to handle. Leonbergers may be active dogs at any age! Be mindful and make sure your dog's golden years are not marred by a new canine that wants to play in a way your older dog can't anymore. Leonbergers are more likely to understand limits and boundaries faster than many other breeds, but you want to minimize how annoyed your older dog is while your puppy is learning those boundaries.

Dog Aggression and Territorial Behavior

Leonbergers may exhibit a level of dominance or aggression toward dogs they don't know, but usually, this is only a concern when they aren't properly socialized. This is one of the primary reasons why you should never let your Leonberger off-leash (the other being they may be a bit too excited and probably won't return because there is too much to explore if they are off-leash). (Details on how to train your Leonberger are discussed in Chapter 13.)

There are two types of aggression you should watch for:

- Dominance aggression is when your dog wants to show control over another animal or person. This kind of aggression can be seen in the following behaviors and in reaction to anyone going near the Leonberger's belongings (like toys or a food bowl):
    - Growling
    - Nipping
    - Snapping

This is the behavior that the pack leader uses to warn others not to touch their stuff. If you see this reaction in your Leonberger while around you, a family member, or another pet, you must intervene immediately. Correct him by saying, "No," then lavish him with praise when the behavior stops. You must consistently intervene whenever your Leonberger behaves in this manner.

Do not leave your Leonberger alone with other people, dogs, or animals as long as any dominance aggression is exhibited. If you are not there to intervene, your dog will push boundaries and will likely try to show his dominance over those around him. Never train your Leonberger to react aggressively!

Once you are sure this behavior has been eliminated, you can leave your current dog and Leonberger alone for short periods of time. You should remain in another room or somewhere in close proximity but out of sight. Over time, you can leave your pets alone when you get the mail; then, try leaving them when you run errands or longer tasks. Eventually, you will be able to safely leave your Leonberger alone with other dogs.

Photo Courtesy
of Brigette Parmenter

Feeding Time Practices

Your Leonberger puppy will be fed in his puppy space, so mealtime will not be a problem in the beginning. However, by the end of the first year, you should be able to have all of your dogs eating in the same area, and that requires some planning and preparation.

The following are suggestions for feeding your puppy when the other dogs are present; this will reduce the chance of territorial behavior:

- Feed your Leonberger at the same time as the other dogs but in a different room. Keeping them separated will let your Leonberger eat without distractions or feeling that your other dogs will eat what is in his bowl. Make sure to feed your Leonberger in the same room each time while the other dogs eat in their established areas.

- Keep your Leonberger and other dogs in their areas until they finish eating their food. Some dogs have a tendency to leave food in the bowl. Don't let them. They need to finish everything because all food bowls will be removed as soon as the dogs finish eating. If food is left, get the bowl off the ground.

- Make sure you have someone near your Leonberger so that the dog learns not to growl at people near the bowl. This will help reduce stress when other dogs are around the food. If your dog demonstrates any aggression, immediately correct him by saying, "No," then give praise when the behavior stops. Do not play with the food bowl, and make sure none of the kids play with it. Your dog needs to know that no one is going to try to steal his food.

- Over the course of a couple of weeks, move your dogs closer together while eating. For example, you can feed your current dog on one side of the door near the doorway and the Leonberger on the opposite side.

- After a month or two, you can feed the dogs in the same room but with some distance between them. If your Leonberger starts to exhibit protective behavior with the other dogs, correct the Leonberger, then praise him when he stops the behavior.

Eventually, you can start feeding the dogs close to one another. This can take weeks to months to accomplish, depending on the age of the Leonberger. A puppy will need less time because he will be socialized with the dogs from an early age, making him less wary. That does not mean he won't display territorial behavior. Yet, it likely won't take long for him to start to feel comfortable eating near the rest of the pack.

For adult dogs, this process could take longer, and you should not rush it. Let your dog learn to feel comfortable eating before you make changes, even small ones. Dogs of any breed can be protective of their food, depending on their past history. Before your dog will eat peacefully, he must be assured that his protective behavior is not necessary around other dogs. That means letting his confidence and comfort level build at his own pace.

CHAPTER 9
The First Few Weeks

The initial excitement from the homecoming isn't going to fade so much as be replaced by the reality of having a new puppy or dog in your home. It's a lot of work, especially during the first week as you try to train your dog while making sure he feels comfortable in his new surroundings. Leaving their previous home, even for a rescue dog, is going to make the dog apprehensive about being somewhere new. There are a lot of things to do (and some things to avoid) to help your dog ease into the new environment and really bring out his fun-loving, enthusiastic, and sometimes mischievous personality. Over time, that personality will come out and change as your dog ages, but during that first week, it is about helping your dog feel comfortable enough to not be wary of the new setting.

As you start to settle into the new routine with your new Leonberger, it's going to be emotional, especially as everyone learns how best to interact with your newest family member. Once the initial apprehension fades, Leonbergers will begin to settle into the new pattern. With their intelligence, Leonbergers will likely quickly understand their new surroundings as they learn that this is their new home. When your dog is not sleeping, you may find yourself feeling that you can't get a moment's rest—but in a fun and entertaining way. The bond you and your Leonberger form in those early days will be important in establishing the relationship you have over the years.

By the end of the first month, your pup should be sleeping through the night. House-training can be very easy when it is done right, but without the right approach, it can be a real chore. Having a great breeder who starts the process will further speed up how quickly your little one learns. You will want to monitor your Leonberger, though, and never let a puppy or dog out of the dedicated area alone during that first week, and probably a good bit longer.

The first month is when you really need to start paying attention to your puppy's emerging personality. As with all intelligent breeds, the key is to remain consistent when it comes to training. That means everyone should be consistent, including the kids. Always use what you learn about your puppy's personality to encourage good behavior!

Photo Courtesy of Paul Sackett & Jackie Sarino

Setting the Rules and Sticking to Them

The Leonberger is an intelligent breed, so if they see that people are willing to compromise, they are going to exploit that as much as possible, and that is far more reckless with a large dog than a small one. This is a dog that can pull carts, so if you don't train your Leonberger how to walk well on a leash, you may find yourself getting pulled off your feet. A good rule for any breed, but especially for larger dogs, is to always set the rules and a schedule and don't allow any deviation. This goes for both your dog and your kids, regardless of the age of the dog or child. You don't want your older children or teens undoing your hard work by letting the new Leonberger out of the puppy's dedicated area to roam around. Make sure everyone knows that the rules apply to everyone.

Your puppy needs to understand the rules and to know you and your family mean them, even if the dog really doesn't like what you are saying. Once your canine learns to follow your commands, there will still be times when he will refuse to obey. That is nearly a certainty. However, he will be much more likely to listen when he knows you are in control.

Do not allow yourself or anyone in your family to think that making an exception is all right, no matter how cute those eyes are. Once a Leonberger realizes that certain rules are negotiable, it will be incredibly difficult to teach him otherwise. The best reward is positive reinforcement, not breaking the rules.

Photo Courtesy of Angela Cairns

Establish a No Jumping and No Mouthing Policy

No matter how cute your puppy might be, you definitely want to start training your dog not to jump up on people because once your dog reaches his full height, he will be able to knock people off their feet. If not properly trained, a Leonberger may jump up on you in greeting, and this can be very bad if the dog tries to jump on little children. Such a sturdy build means the dog can easily knock over a toddler unintentionally. You have the responsibility of ensuring that your dog and children learn how to play properly. For your Leonberger, this means no jumping up on people.

Nor do you want a puppy to feel it is all right to mouth you because when your dog is fully grown, his mouth is going to be enormous. Any games that involve biting or nipping should always be avoided. You do not want your Leonberger to ever think that nipping is all right. This will be very difficult if you don't enforce the rule right from the beginning.

NIPPING

Though they aren't generally aggressive, Leonbergers (or any dog) are likely to nip under two conditions. Most situations when dogs nip are related to these two scenarios.

- One of the triggers for nipping is overstimulation. This can be one sign your puppy is too tired to keep playing or training, and you should put him to bed.

- Another trigger could be that your canine has too much energy. If this is the case, take your puppy outside to burn off some of his excess energy. At the same time, be careful not to over-exercise the puppy.

You need to be vigilant and immediately let your puppy know nipping is not acceptable. Some people recommend using a water spritzer bottle and spraying the puppy while saying, "No," after nipping. This is one of the few times when punishment may be effective, and it is probably essential. Remember—make sure your dog does not associate the spraying with anything other than his nipping. He needs to understand that he is getting sprayed because he is nipping someone and that this is not acceptable behavior.

Always firmly tell your puppy, "No," whenever he is nipping, even if it is during playtime. You should also pull away and loudly say, "Ouch!" to let your puppy know his teeth are hurting you. This will help to establish the idea that nipping is bad and is never rewarded.

Photo Courtesy
of MacKenzie Jones

CHEWING

All puppies chew to relieve the pain of teething. Whether your dog is chewing on your furniture or clothing, be sure to discourage this behavior as quickly as possible:

- Make sure you have toys for your Leonberger (whether an adult or a puppy) so that you can teach him what objects are acceptable for chewing. Having a lot of available toys and rotating those toys out will give your puppy or dog several options.

- If your puppy is teething, either refrigerate a couple of toys so that they are cold or give your puppy frozen carrots. The cold will help to numb the pain. Teething usually starts at between three and four months old, and it usually ends by eight months. You want to get toys that will be safe for your dog's teeth.

- Toys that are made either of hard rubber or hard nylon are best, particularly Kongs with kibble in them. You can even fill them with water and freeze them, which will give your puppy something cool to soothe the pain of teething.

For the most part, keeping an eye on your dog when he is not in his designated space will help you quickly see when he is chewing on things he shouldn't. When this happens, firmly say, "No." If your dog continues to chew, put him back in his space. While he is in the space, make sure he has plenty of toys to chew on.

If you decide to use chew deterrents, such as bitter training sprays, be aware some dogs will not care if an item tastes bad—they will chew on it anyway. If you apply these deterrents, do not leave your dog alone and expect him to stop chewing. You should watch your dog's reaction before trusting that the bad habit is broken. Since some Leonbergers have separation anxiety, you should eliminate the chewing problem as quickly as possible; this will allow your pup to roam freely around your home.

JUMPING

As noted earlier, Leonbergers must not be allowed to jump up on other people or animals. Use the following steps when you have a visitor. If you can, get someone who is willing to help because that will make training that much easier:

1. Put a leash on the dog when the person knocks on the door or rings the bell. The arrival of someone will invariably excite most dogs, especially puppies.

2. Let the person in, but do not approach the visitor until your pup calms down.

3. Be effusive in your praise when the puppy keeps all four paws on the ground.

4. If the puppy jumps up on the visitor, the visitor should turn his body and ignore the dog. Don't verbally correct the dog. Being completely ignored will be far more of a deterrent than any words you can say.

5. Give your dog something to hold in his mouth if he does not settle down. Sometimes dogs just need a task to reduce their excitement. A stuffed animal or a ball is an ideal distraction, even if your dog drops it.

6. At this point, the visitor can get low and pet your dog. Having someone on his level will make your Leonberger feel he is being included. It also lets him sniff the visitor's face, which is part of a proper greeting to a dog. If your visitor is willing to help, this acknowledgment can prevent your pup from further jumping since he already feels safe with the person who is at his level.

Reward-Based Training Versus Discipline-Based Training

With an intelligent breed like the Leonberger, it is much more efficient to train your puppy using rewards than with punishments. This will be a particular challenge as puppies can be exuberant and are easily distracted. It is important to remember that your puppy is young, so you need to keep your temper and learn when a break from training is needed. Since Leonbergers are more interested in pleasing their people, positive attention can be incredibly effective in getting your dog to listen.

The following lists several critical training aspects you will need to address during the first month:

- House-training (Chapter 9)
- Crate training (Chapter 6)
- Barking (Chapter 11)

Find out how much house-training was completed by the breeder. The best breeders may teach puppies one or two commands before the puppy goes home with you. If this is the case, keep using those same commands with your puppy so that the early training is not lost. This information can help you establish the right tone of voice to use with your puppy since he will already know what the words mean and how to react to them.

How Long Is Too Long to Be Left Home Alone?

In the beginning, your dog should spend only a brief period of time in the crate while you are gone. Leonbergers have literally been companions since they were first bred, so they do not like to be left home alone. This is why it is best to make sure they have a companion. As your dog becomes house-trained and trustworthy, you should allow him to leave the crate while you are gone so that he doesn't feel he is being punished.

Your new companion will not do well trapped in a crate for hours at a time. That said, in an emergency, dogs can be all right in a crate for up to eight hours without a person as long as you have made sure to allow the dog to burn off energy first.

You also need to find some good mental games that will keep your pup occupied while you are gone. Brain games can keep your dog happily occupied while you are away, and having another dog can provide stimulation (though you may want to make sure to tire them both out before leaving).

HELPFUL TIP
Bedsharing

The first few nights with a new puppy can be a trying experience for both you and your dog. Many new dog owners are tempted to ease the transition by putting the puppy in bed with them. Aside from the inherent safety risks of placing a puppy in bed, including the risk of falling, it's better for you and for your Leonberger to establish a safe sleeping space for your puppy. Though initially small, Leonbergers are a giant breed and may quickly grow too big to share your bed! If you want to keep your puppy close for the first few nights, try placing a crate within sight in your bedroom.

Don't Overdo It – Physically or Mentally

> *One of my biggest issues is that Leos (or any giant breed) take time to physically develop. Remember, they are about one pound at birth and over 20 pounds at eight weeks. Most will be pushing 100 pounds at six months. Their joints can take over 12 months to develop and close. We recommend no tile floors, few stairs, and rugs on wooden floors. Often we find people exercise their Leos too much the first year and can cause permanent damage.*
>
> BRENDA FORD & MARY ANN FARENZENA
> *Leos from the Lion's Den*

As an adult, your Leonberger will probably be highly active. As a puppy, your Leonberger will go from sleeping to being rambunctious to sleeping again, all within a brief period of time. A tired puppy is a lot like a tired toddler; you have to keep the little guy from becoming exhausted or from overworking those short little legs (while they are still short). You need to be careful about harming your puppy's growing bones. Your pup is probably going to think that sleep is unnecessary, no matter how tired he is. It is up to you to read the signs that tell you when to stop all activities and take a break or put your pup to bed.

You should train your dog in increments of time—only for the amount of time that he can handle. Don't push your puppy's training past his con-centration level, and don't discourage your adult dog by using commands that are too advanced. If you continue training your puppy past his energy levels, the lessons learned are not going to be the ones you want to teach your dog. At this age, training sessions don't need to be long; they just need to be consistent.

Walks will be much shorter during the first month. When you go outside, stay within a few blocks of home. Don't worry—by the month's end, your puppy will have more stamina, and you can enjoy longer walks with your new friend. You can also do a bit of walking on the leash in the yard if your puppy has lots of extra energy. Puppies have a tendency to attack their leash while walking because it is a distraction from running freely. Taking walks will also help your Leonberger learn how to behave on the leash.

Just because your puppy can't endure long walks initially doesn't mean he won't have plenty of energy. Daily exercise will be essential, with the caveats that you need to make sure your puppy isn't doing too much too soon and that he doesn't get too hot. Staying active will not only keep him healthy, but it will also keep him mentally stimulated. You will quickly realize how sedentary your "non-puppy life" has been because you will be on the move the entire time your puppy is awake!

PART 3
TRAINING AND ACTIVITIES

CHAPTER 10
House-training

This chapter covers one of the least enjoyable but absolutely essential aspects of having a dog—house-training. Leonbergers are easy to train when it comes to nearly everything else, so you just need to treat house-training with the same kind of patience and consistency that you apply to other types of training. This does tend to be more difficult because we want to punish "bad behavior," not stopping to think that what a dog is doing is natural. Keep in mind that your Leonberger isn't misbehaving or intentionally disobeying you; he is learning where to go to the restroom, which is a lot harder than learning how to sit. To speed up the process, be patient and praise your dog when he goes in the right place.

The recommended age to start house-training a Leonberger is between 12 and 16 weeks. Before that, you can start showing him other dogs going outside to relieve themselves, but Leonbergers won't have enough bladder and bowel control to be consistent until they are about 12 weeks old.

While you are trying to train the dog where to use the bathroom, you will almost certainly see your dog trying to decide if he should listen to you. All it takes is one time when you allow yourself to be distracted, and you can turn house-training into an incredibly difficult chore. But if you

HELPFUL TIP
Puppy-Proofing

Leonberger puppies can start house-training as young as eight weeks. This training can take a few weeks, but you can speed the process up by taking steps to puppy proof. Keeping your puppy close during those crucial weeks of house-training can help to ensure that your dog doesn't have any unwanted accidents by allowing you to observe the signs that your dog needs to go! Therefore, keeping the puppy close is essential. In addition, puppy-proofing your house by utilizing baby gates, playpens, and closing doors to spare rooms can keep your Leonberger from wandering out of sight to where you could miss important cues.

can keep your focus while remaining consistent and firm, your Leonberger should be trained by the time he's six months old.

Staying focused when you have your dog outside for a restroom break isn't necessarily enough; if you fail to keep a constant eye on your puppy when he is exploring inside your home, be prepared for a lot of messes. Puppies will sneak off to use the bathroom inside if you let your attention stray. Leonbergers can be stubborn, so you cannot give them any chance to get away with ever using your home as a bathroom.

This is when learning to be firm and consistent is really going to count, and sticking to the rules will be absolutely essential. You will also need to remain calm and patient; getting upset will only reinforce undesirable behavior. The best tool in house-training a potentially stubborn breed is to set a schedule and stick to it—no deviations! Once your dog realizes you are staying focused and that you will get him outside for a break, he will accept that rule and do what he's supposed to do.

Leashing your Leonberger to go outside can help show your puppy where and when to go to the bathroom—even in your yard. However, there will still be challenges.

The following is a list of rules to apply when house-training:

- Never let the puppy roam the house alone—he should always be in his dedicated puppy space when you are not watching him. No Leonberger wants to spend a lot of time in a soiled crate, so being in his crate is a deterrent from doing his business there when you are not around. He may not feel the same way about other areas of your home if he is free to wander.

- Give your puppy constant, easy access to his designated bathroom spaces. You will need to make frequent trips outside with your puppy as he learns where to do his business.

- When you go outside, put a leash on your puppy to make a point of where in the yard you want him to use the bathroom.

Always begin with a training plan; then, be even stricter with yourself than you are with your puppy when keeping the schedule. You are the key to your puppy's learning!

Photo Courtesy
of Paul Sackett & Jackie Sarino

Inside or Outside – House-training Options and Considerations

If your breeder has already started the house-training process, make sure to coordinate your training so that you pick up where the breeder left off. Having someone who really knows how to house-train a dog can give you a huge leg up on the whole endeavor—take it if you can get it!

The following is a list of house-training options for your puppy:

- Pee pads – You should have several around the home for training, including in the puppy's area but as far from his bed as possible.
- Regular outings – Organize these outings based on your puppy's sleeping and eating schedule.
- Rewards – You can use treats in the beginning but quickly shift to praise.

Setting a Schedule

You need to keep an eye on your puppy and always follow his meals, before and after sleep, and before and after being in his crate with house-training sessions. Watch for cues like sniffing and circling, which are two common signs a puppy exhibits when searching for a place to go potty. Start tailoring your schedule around your puppy's unique needs. Puppies have small bladders and little control in the early days—so at this time, it isn't stubbornness but ability that is making it difficult for your puppy to follow your directions.

If you train your pup to do his business inside, you need a designated space in the puppy's area for a clean pee pad. Pee pads are better than newspapers and can absorb more. Make sure you change the pads regularly so that your puppy does not get accustomed to having waste nearby. Even if you use pee pads, you should plan to transition your dog to doing his business outdoors as quickly as possible.

Choosing a Location

A designated bathroom space will make the house-training experience easier because your Leonberger will associate one area of the yard with that specific purpose. Having him use one spot every time will also make cleanup simpler, and you will be able to use the entire yard instead of having to worry about stepping in dog waste.

The perfect time to train your puppy to go to the bathroom is when you go out for walks. Between walks and using the yard, your puppy will come to see the leash as a sign that it is time to relieve his bladder, which could become a Pavlovian response.

Do not send your puppy outside alone and assume he has done what you want him to do. He needs to understand the purpose of going outside is to go to the bathroom. Until there are no more accidents in the house, you need to be sure your puppy is not losing focus. With a breed like the Leonberger, it is best to always verify that your little fellow follows through. If it is too hot or cold outside, and you don't make sure he takes care of business, you run the risk that he will take advantage of that lack of supervision to pretend he has done his business just so he can get back inside faster. Then accidents are nearly guaranteed, even if you thought that your dog was fully house-trained.

Keyword Training

All training should include keywords, even house-training. You and all family members should consistently use keywords when house-training your dog. If you have paired an adult with a child, the adult should be the one using the keyword during training.

To avoid confusing your puppy, be careful not to select words that you often use inside the home. Use a phrase like, "Get busy" to let your puppy know it's time to do his business. Do not use words like "bathroom" or "potty" because these words are sometimes used in casual conversation, which could trigger a desire in your dog to go to the bathroom. "Get busy" is not a phrase most people use in their daily routine, so it is not something you are likely to say unless you want your puppy to go to the bathroom outside.

Once your puppy learns to use the bathroom based on the command, make sure he finishes before offering praise or rewards.

Photo Courtesy
of Maryann Zukowski

Reward Good Behavior with
Positive Reinforcement

Leonbergers are incredibly receptive to positive reinforcement, making it highly effective for all kinds of training (not just house-training). In the beginning, take a few pieces of kibble with you when you are teaching your puppy where to go, both inside and outside the home. Learning you are the one in charge will help teach your Leonberger to look to you for cues and instructions.

Part of being consistent with training means lavishing the little guy with praise whenever your puppy does the right thing. Use a leash to gently lead your puppy to his bathroom area, with no stops in between. It will gradually become obvious to your Leonberger that this is where he should go to use the bathroom. Once you get outside, encourage your pup to go only when you get to the place in the yard that is intended for his bathroom spot. As soon as he does his business, give him immediate and very enthusiastic praise. Pet your puppy as you talk, and let the little guy know just how good the action was. Once the praise is done, return inside immediately. This is not playtime. You want your puppy to associate certain outings with designated potty time.

While praise is incredibly effective with Leonbergers, you can also give your puppy a treat after a few successful trips outside. Definitely do not make treats a habit after each trip because you do not want your Leonberger to expect one every time he does his business. The lesson is to go outside, not to receive a treat every time.

The best way to house-train in the first couple of months is to go out every hour or two, even during the night. Set an alarm to wake yourself during the night so that you remember to take the puppy outside. Use the leash to keep the focus on using the bathroom, give the same enthusiastic praise, then immediately return inside and go back to bed. It is difficult, but your Leonberger will get the hang of it a lot faster if there isn't a lengthy period between potty breaks. Over time, the pup will need to go outside less frequently.

Cleaning Up

Once a dog goes to the bathroom in your home, that odor will remain there for other dogs to smell, even if it's not detectable to your own nose after you've cleaned the area thoroughly. Your Leonberger might take

Photo Courtesy
of Alex and Cheryl O'Brien

any lingering odor as a sign that the spot is an acceptable place to use the bathroom.

This means you have to be very diligent about handling accidents:

- Clean up any messes in the house as soon as you find them.
- In areas where your dog has an accident, thoroughly clean the spot so that there is no remaining scent.

Spend a bit of time researching what kinds of cleaner you want to use, whether generic or holistic. For example, you will probably want to get a product with an enzyme cleaner. Enzymes help to remove stains by speeding up the chemical reaction of the cleaner with the stain. They also help to remove the smell faster, which reduces the odds your dog will continue to go to the bathroom in the same place. If your Leonberger is properly trained, he will feel no need to mark his territory, but you should also discourage other dogs from claiming areas around your property.

If your Leonberger has an accident, it is important to refrain from punishing the puppy. Punishment simply teaches your dog to hide his mess or to be stealthier about when he does his business inside. Accidents are not a reason to punish. If they happen often, it is really more of a reflection of your training and your schedule than on the puppy. However, even the best trainers can tell you accidents are pretty much an inevitability. When it happens, tell your puppy, "No! Potty outside!" and clean up the mess immediately. Once you have finished cleaning the mess, take the puppy outside. It isn't likely that he will need to go potty again, but it is worth the attempt in case he still has a little left.

Pay attention to when these accidents happen, and determine if there is a commonality between them. Perhaps you need to add an extra trip outside during the day for your puppy, or you should make a change in his walking schedule. Or maybe there is something that is startling your dog and causing an accident.

CHAPTER 11

Training Your Leonberger

Leonbergers are considered moderately easy to train, a task that is made much easier by using positive reinforcement, and that doesn't mean giving your pup a lot of extra treats. Positive attention and extra play are fantastic rewards for a loving dog like the Leonberger. As they are dogs that do not like negative emotions and are very sensitive to any negativity, it is best not to agitate them and make them feel upset because that will make them less likely to understand or do what you want.

It is absolutely essential to ensure that your Leonberger learns the basic commands covered in these chapters for his protection and for that of your visitors. Given his size, a Leonberger can get carried away and knock people over without any understanding of how dangerous his actions are.

Photo Courtesy of Leon Gerrits

Early Training is a Must

> **"**
>
> *Leos are very smart and tend to not like repetition. They prefer to perform when it is their idea, so sometimes training can be a challenge. Make training sessions fun and exciting, and change up the routine often for more success. Short, quick sessions tend to bring more results than longer, mundane sessions.*
>
> ERIN ANDERSEN
> *High Hopes Newfoundlands and Leonbergers*
> **"**

All large dogs require early training because of the risks they pose if they don't learn how to behave. From knocking people over to literally running over children, large dogs are more likely to accidentally harm others. It can be difficult to stay composed when a dog keeps jumping up on people because most people don't know how to deal with this kind of behavior in an effective way. The natural reaction is to give a dog attention, even if it is to try to convince him to stay down. Training him early, before he spends much time outside with others, will help you to get some of the bad behaviors worked out. Given how different Leonbergers look from most other breeds, you'll find that a lot of people will approach your dog. Your Leonberger will probably be just as curious about them, so you want to make sure that you are able to keep all four of his paws on the ground during social interactions.

Best Practices and Benefits to Keep in Mind before You Start

> **"**
>
> *They are very smart and will do an activity once for you. The second time you ask, they will do it again but will look at you like you are crazy. The third time you ask, they will know you are crazy, ignore you, and lie down.*
>
> SUE HERMAN
> *Water's Edge Leonbergers*
> **"**

In the early days, be prepared to keep your frustration levels in check. Your dog has to be convinced that you are in charge and that you mean business—and he needs to know the reward for that is a lot of fun. If you take out your frustration on your Leonberger, you are teaching him that training isn't fun. Whether you bring a puppy or an adult dog into your home, he has to learn the boundaries in a way that is safe and shows patience, just like with teaching a child. If you take a few minutes to watch training videos of Leonbergers from the beginning, that will give you a good idea of what you could be in for when you start to train your newest family member.

Just remember—being firm, consistent, and patient will go a long way. Don't let that adorable face sway you from getting your pup to do what you

Photo Courtesy of Don and Brenda Gamble

instruct him to do. He will be just as happy a little way down the road if you stick to it now. And that happy face when playing with you is priceless.

Always make the early training sessions short, no matter how old your dog is. Those training sessions are as much about learning how your Leonberger will respond to training as they are about actually training your dog. Puppies won't have the ability to keep focus like an adult, so a short session is ideal for keeping them from learning to ignore you. Adult dogs are going to be suspicious of you (though you

FUN FACT
Moose the Therapy Dog

A 110-pound Leonberger in Wisconsin serves as a therapy dog at Saint A's, a nonprofit organization in Milwaukee serving children and families. His name is Bullwinkle Moose, Moose for short, and he works with his owner, youth counselor Kay Bobb, and the young boys under her supervision, most of whom are seven to 10 years old. Many of the children who interact with Moose are trauma survivors. Leonbergers are popular therapy dogs because of their gentle disposition and love of children.

may also get an adult that is already familiar with training, which could make training a little easier). And odds are, you are going to be quite tired by the end of those sessions—you'll be just as relieved as your pup to be done. As long as you are firm and consistent during those early sessions, keeping them short is in everyone's best interest.

Training will be slow going in the beginning, as your dog will be quite excited about the interaction. Don't take this as an indication of your puppy's interest levels—it's more indicative of his inexperience. If you are patient with your pup from the start, you will find it will pay off later.

Training is as important as socialization, and it can make general excursions easier; more importantly, training could be a way of saving your dog's life. Understanding commands might prevent your dog from running into the street, responding to provocations from other dogs, or acting territorial.

Training can also really benefit your relationship with your pup because it is a wonderful way to bond. This dedicated time together helps you understand your puppy's developing personality as you learn what kind of reward will work best for other tasks. Be sure your Leonberger is well-trained so you can enjoy a full range of activities together—from picnics to outings in the park!

Choosing the Right Reward

The right reward for a Leonberger will ultimately be love and affection because these dogs adore their people. Treats are the easiest way of keying a puppy into the idea that performing tricks is good behavior, but ultimately you want your little one to follow commands without expecting food. Soon, you will need to switch to a reward that is a secondary reinforcer. Praise, additional playtime, and extra petting are all fantastic rewards for your Leonberger. Your dog will probably follow you around until you decide to just sit back and relax. Plopping down to watch a movie and letting your puppy sit with you is a great reward after an intense training session.

Make sure you switch from treats to a different kind of positive reward as early as possible. Since many Leonbergers love their toys, you don't have to rely solely on treats as a method of praise.

If you would like your Leonberger to connect positive feedback with a sound, you can use a clicker. This training tool is relatively inexpensive and should be used at the same time as you praise your puppy or dog. Clickers are not necessary, but some trainers find them useful.

Name Recognition

Leos want to please their humans, but they are not as avid about it as perhaps a German Shepherd or a Sheltie would be. When training your puppy, remember to keep any lessons fun and short.

PEGGY ATCHLEY
Great Northern Leonbergers

Over time, many of us create different names for our dogs. Nicknames can be used later. However, before you can train a dog, you have to make sure he understands his real name.

The following list provides some name recognition suggestions:

1. Get some treats and show one to your dog.

2. Say the dog's name and immediately say, "Yes." (Your dog should be looking at you when you speak.) Then, give your dog a treat.

3. Wait 10 seconds, then show your dog a treat and repeat step two.

Photo Courtesy
of Aare Oopik

Sessions shouldn't last longer than about five minutes because your dog will lose focus or interest. Name recognition is something you can do several times each day. After you have done this for five to 10 sessions, the training will change a bit:

1. Wait until your dog isn't paying attention to you.

2. Call your dog. If he has a leash on, give it a gentle tug to get your dog's attention.

3. Say, "Yes," and give the dog a treat when he looks at you.

During this time, do not speak your dog's name when you correct him or for any reason other than name recognition. This is because, in the beginning, you need to get the dog to associate his name only with something positive, like treats. This will more quickly program your dog to listen to you no matter what else is going on around him.

It is likely that your Leonberger will not require a lot of time before he recognizes his name. Repetition while looking at your pup is a great way to speed up the learning process.

Essential Commands

There are seven basic commands that all dogs should know (Sit, Down, Stay, Come, Leave It, Drop It, and Heel). These commands are the basis for a happy and enjoyable relationship with your dog, as well as giving you a way to keep your dog safe and out of trouble. Then there are some commands that are incredibly helpful, like "Off" if you don't want pets on the furniture and "Quiet" for a noisy dog.

Train your puppy to do the commands in the order they appear in this chapter. The last two commands are optional since you may allow your dog to be on the furniture, and you may not mind a vocal canine. Since dogs sit often, "Sit" is the easiest command to teach, making it the best starting point. Teaching "Leave It" and "Drop It" is much more difficult and usually requires the puppy to fight an instinct or a desire. Consider how often you give in to something you want, even when you know you shouldn't! That's pretty much what your puppy is facing.

"Quiet" can be another difficult command, as dogs (particularly puppies) tend to bark in response to their surroundings. Some puppies do grow out of the constantly barking stage. If you finish all the other commands and find that your dog is still a bit too noisy for your home, you can then start training him to be quiet, though you will need to determine just when you want him to be quiet and when you want him to bark (like when someone is outside your home). This will take some consideration on your part.

The following are some basic steps to use during training:

1. Include everyone in the home in the Leonberger training. The puppy must learn to listen to everyone in the household and not just one or two people. A set training schedule may only involve a couple of people in the beginning, especially if you have children. There should always be an adult present when training, but including a child will help reinforce the idea that the puppy must listen to everyone in the house. It is also an effective way for a parent to monitor a child's interaction with the puppy so that everyone plays in a way that is safe and follows the rules.

2. To get started, select an area where you and your puppy have no other distractions, including noise. Leave your phone and other devices out of range so that you are able to keep your attention on the puppy.

3. Stay happy and excited about the training. Your puppy will pick up on your enthusiasm and will focus better because of it.

4. Be consistent and firm as you teach.

5. Bring special treats to the first few training sessions, such as pieces of chicken or small treats.

Sit

Start to teach the command "Sit" when your puppy is around eight weeks old.

Once you settle into your quiet training location:

1. Hold out a treat.
2. Move the treat over your puppy's head. This will make the puppy move back.
3. Say, "Sit" as the puppy's haunches touch the floor.

Having a second person around to demonstrate this with your puppy will be helpful, as the person can sit to show the dog what you mean.

Wait until your puppy starts to sit down and say, "Sit" as he sits. If your puppy finishes sitting down, give praise. Naturally, this will make your puppy excited and wiggly, so it may take a bit of time before he will want to sit again. When your puppy calms down, repeat the process.

It's going to take more than a couple of sessions for the puppy to fully connect your words with actions. Commands are something completely new to your little companion. Once your puppy has demonstrated mastery of the command "Sit," start teaching "Down."

Down

Repeat the same process when teaching this command as you did for Sit:

1. Tell your dog to Sit.
2. Hold out the treat.
3. Lower the treat to the floor with your dog sniffing at it. Allow your pup to lick the treat, but if he stands up, start over.
4. Say, "Down" as the puppy's elbows touch the floor (make sure to say it as he does the action to help him associate the word with the action), then give praise while rewarding your puppy with the treat.

It will probably take a little less time to teach this command. Wait until your puppy has mastered "Down" before moving on to "Stay."

Stay

"Stay" is a vital command to teach because it can keep your puppy from running across a street or from running at someone who is nervous or scared of dogs. It is important your dog has mastered Sit and Down before you teach Stay. Learning this command is going to be more difficult since it is not something your puppy does naturally.

Be prepared for this command to take a bit longer to teach:

1. Tell your puppy to either Sit or Stay.

2. As you do this, place your hand in front of the puppy's face.

3. Wait until the puppy stops trying to lick your hand before you continue.

4. When the puppy settles down, take a step away. If your puppy is not moving, say, "Stay," and give a treat and some praise.

Giving your puppy the reward indicates the command is over, but you also need to indicate the command is complete. The puppy has to learn to stay until you say it is okay to leave the spot. Once you give the okay to move, do not give treats. The command Come should not be used as the okay word, as it is a command used for something else.

Repeat these steps, taking more steps further away from the puppy after a successful command.

Once your puppy understands Stay when you move away, start training him to stay even if you are not moving. Extend the amount of time required for the puppy to stay in one spot so that he understands Stay ends with the "Okay" command.

When you feel that your puppy has Stay mastered, start training the puppy to "Come."

Come

This is a command you can't teach until the puppy has learned the previous commands. Before you start the training session, decide if you want to use "Come" or "Come Here." Be consistent in the words you use.

This command is important for the same reason as the previous one; if you are around people who are nervous around dogs, or if you encounter a wild animal or other distraction, this command will snap your puppy's attention back to you:

1. Leash the puppy.

2. Tell the puppy to Stay.

3. Move away from the puppy.

4. Say the command you will use for Come, and give a gentle tug on the leash toward you.

Repeat these steps, building a larger distance between you and the puppy. Once the puppy seems to understand, remove the leash, and start at a close distance. If your puppy doesn't seem to understand the command, give some visual clues about what you want. For example, you can pat your leg or snap your fingers. As soon as your puppy comes running over to you, offer a reward.

Leave It

This is a difficult training command, but you need to train your dog to "Leave It" for when you are out on a walk and want him to ignore other people or dogs.

1. Let your dog see that you have treats in your hand, then close your hand. Your fist should be close enough for your dog to sniff the treat.

2. Say, "Leave it" when your dog starts to sniff your hand.

3. Say, "Yes," and give your dog a treat when he turns his head away from the treats. Initially, this will probably take a while, as your dog will want those treats. Don't continue to say, "Leave it," as your dog should not be learning that you will give a command more than once. You want him to learn he must do what you say the first time, which is why treats are recommended in the beginning. If a minute or more passes after giving the command, you can then issue it again, but make sure your canine is focused on you and not distracted.

These sessions should only last about five minutes. Your dog will need time to learn this command as you are teaching him to ignore something he naturally wants. When he looks away and stops sniffing when you say, "Leave it," you can move on to more advanced versions of the training:

1. Leave your hand open so that your dog can see the treats.

2. Say, "Leave it" when your dog starts to show interest. This will probably be immediate since your hand will be open, so be prepared.

    a. Close your fist if your dog continues to sniff or gets near the treats in your hand.

b. Give your dog a treat from your other hand if he stops.

Repeat these steps until your dog finally stops trying to sniff the treats. When your dog seems to have learned this command, move on to the most difficult version of this command.

1. Place treats on the ground, or let your dog see you hide them. Then, stay close to those treats.

2. Say, "Leave it" when your dog starts to show interest in sniffing the treats.

   a. Place a hand over the treats if he doesn't listen.

   b. Give a treat if your dog does listen.

From here, you can start training while standing further from the treat with your dog leashed so you can stop him if needed. Then, start to use other things that your dog loves, such as a favorite toy or another tempting treat that you don't usually give him.

Drop It

This is going to be one of the most difficult commands to teach because it goes against both your puppy's instincts and interests. Your puppy wants to keep whatever he has, so you are going to have to offer him something better instead. It is essential to teach the command early, as your Leonberger could be very destructive in the early days. Furthermore, this command could save your pooch's life. When you are out for a walk, he will probably lunge at objects that look like food. However, once he has mastered this command, he will drop anything he picks up.

Start with a toy and a large treat that your dog cannot eat in a matter of seconds, such as a rawhide. Make sure the treat you have is one your puppy does not get very often so that there is motivation to drop the toy or big treat.

1. Give your puppy the toy or large treat. If you want to use a clicker, too, pair it with the exciting treat you will use to help convince your puppy to drop the treat.

2. Show your puppy the exciting treat.

3. Say, "Drop it," and when he drops the treat or toy, tell him, "Good," and hand over the exciting treat while picking up the dropped item.

4. Repeat this immediately after your puppy finishes eating the exciting treat.

You will need to keep reinforcing this command for months after it is learned because it is not a natural instinct.

Heel

"Heel" is a command that is incredibly beneficial. It keeps your dog from weaving in front of you on a walk, potentially being a tripping hazard, and gives you a command that will help to distract your dog if a squirrel or other small animal crosses your path. Telling your dog to "heel" if you see the squirrel first can be a good reminder to your dog not to chase the squirrel.

Equally importantly, "heel" is a command that you need to use when socializing your dog. Your Leonberger should know how to heel before you really start socializing him to ensure that your dog is calmer or at least is still listening to you when you approach other people and dogs.

The purpose of this command is to teach your dog to walk by your side. This can be incredibly frustrating and annoying in practice, which is what really leads to people failing to teach this command. When we go outside, we get distracted, or we just want to hurry and get back inside—especially if it is cold, hot, or raining. Failing to be consistent with this command will undermine your efforts to actually teach it. Training in all of the other commands will help you to learn your dog's personality, what works, and the rewards that will keep your Leonberger's attention during training to "heel."

Have some of your dog's favorite treats in a small bag that you can quickly and easily access them. Cut the treats down to a small size (about the size of a penny) because you are going to be giving a lot of these in the early days.

Training will begin inside. This means you will probably want to leash your dog inside, which can lead to excitement if your dog thinks you are going outside. If that happens, calm your dog before you start training. Choose the room with the most space for walking around it; halls can be a good choice since there is typically ample room for walking in a straight line, which will be more like walking outside.

1. Determine which side you want your dog to walk on, then hold a treat up to your chest on the side where you want the dog so that your dog cannot reach it. This will help keep from distracting the dog from listening to your commands. The side you choose should be the side where you want your dog to walk when you go outside; usually, people train dogs to walk on their left side but choose the side that is most comfortable for you.

2. Point to the side you prefer and call the dog's name, then say the word "Heel."

3. Give your puppy a treat as soon as he reaches the correct side and say "yes" or "good." If you also plan to use a clicker, use it as you give your dog the treat. Having the treat on the same side as your dog will keep him from crossing to the wrong side.

4. Move away from your dog, point to the same side, and call his name and say, "Heel."

5. Immediately reward him for coming and standing on the correct side.

Over the next few days, as your dog starts to understand what you want him to do without treats, you can start trying to throw him off by zig-zag-ging or turning to teach him to keep you as a point of reference. When he gets the concept and remains on the correct side, start getting his attention by saying, "Look," and make eye contact. This reinforces that his attention needs to be on you and on staying by your side.

Once your dog is able to do this inside, you can start working on "heel" when you are outside. You want to make sure that your dog understands the command before going outside where there are so many distractions. If your dog is accustomed to being on one side when walking, it will be more automatic for your dog, which will go a long way toward helping your dog stay focused when you move from the controlled home environment to the more chaotic outdoors.

You will need to keep reinforcing this command for months after it is learned because it is not a natural instinct.

Off

This is different from training your dog not to jump on people (Chapter 9). This command is specifically to get your dog off furniture or surfaces that may be dangerous. This is training you will need to do on the fly because you are training your dog to stop an action. This means you have to react to that undesirable action. Having treats on hand will be essential when you see your dog getting up on things you don't want him to be on:

1. Wait for your dog to put his paws on something you don't want him on.

2. Say, "Off," and lure him away with a treat that you keep just out of his reach.

3. Say, "Yes," and give him a treat as soon as his paws are off the surface.

Repeat this every time you see the behavior. It will probably take at least half a dozen times before your dog understands he should not perform the action anymore. Over time, switch from treats to praise or playing with a toy.

Quiet

Leonbergers are not known for their barking. They are more likely to bark if they sense negativity, feel bored or anxious, or feel protective. For the most part, these reasons are not going to result in excessive barking; however, negativity is inevitable, so you may want to take some time to train your dog not to bark, and that will probably be easier with a younger dog since they are more likely to bark.

1. When your puppy barks for no obvious reason, tell him to be quiet and place a treat nearby. It is almost guaranteed your dog will fall silent to sniff the treat.

2. If your dog does fall silent, say, "Good dog" or "Good quiet."

It will not take too long for your puppy to understand "Quiet" means no barking.

If you want your Leonberger to be more of a watchdog, you will need to provide some guidance on when he should bark and when he should not. This will likely be a challenge since they are not prone to barking. A professional can help tailor the approach to training your dog when to bark at people at the door. However, if you want a watchdog or a guard dog, there are a lot of breeds that are better equipped for that than Leonbergers.

Until all of these commands are learned, it is best to avoid other types of advanced training. Between the ages of six and 12 months, you should be able to move on to training your dog to do tricks. Chapter 14 provides more details on tricks and games that your Leonberger may love.

Where to Go from Here

Most dogs will need some additional training so that you can keep them from being overexuberant and reckless. Chapter 13 provides alternatives for helping your dog use up all of his energy, but you need to at least ensure that your dog learns the basic commands. The following classes can help you learn to keep yourself calm so that your training is effective. These classes are really as much for you as for your dog.

Puppy Classes

> *I make sure that my new owners have their pups signed up for at least one puppy class and one beginner obedience class. I tell them to keep in mind that even though the pup is small now, it will grow to be over 100 pounds, and you need to be able to control your dog when out in public. Getting your Leo started in a class is the best way to start socializing in a controlled environment.*
>
> PAULA DEVORE
> *Rev It Up Kennel*

Puppies can begin to go to puppy school as early as six weeks, but you will probably want to wait until your Leonberger has had all of his shots. You will need to set aside an hour or two so that you can research schools near you. Make sure to take the time to read the reviews and see if you can talk to people who have used a particular school or trainer. Trainers should be willing to take the time to talk to you and answer questions as well, so try talking to the people running the school. This is the beginning of obedience training, but you need to be careful around other dogs until your puppy has completed his vaccinations. Talk with your vet about when is an appropriate time to begin classes. Your vet may also be able to recommend good puppy training classes in your area.

The primary purpose of these classes is socialization. Studies show one-third of all puppies have minimal exposure to unfamiliar people and dogs during the first 20 weeks of their life. This can make the outside world pretty scary! The puppy classes give you and your puppy a chance to learn how to meet and greet other people and dogs in a controlled environment. Dogs that attend these classes are much friendlier and are less stressed about such things as large trucks, thunder, loud noises, and unfamiliar visitors. They are also less likely to be nervous or suffer from separation anxiety, a likely issue for a Leonberger.

Puppy classes are also great training for you! The same studies show owners who attend classes learn to react appropriately when a puppy is disobedient or misbehaves. The classes teach you how to train your puppy and how to deal with the emerging headstrong nature of your dog.

Many classes will help you with some of the basic commands, like Sit and Down. Look for a class that also focuses on socialization so that your puppy can get the most out of the instruction.

Obedience Training

After your puppy graduates from puppy school and understands most of the basic commands, you can switch to obedience classes. Some trainers offer at-home obedience training, but if you do this, it's still a good idea to also set aside regular time to socialize your pup at a dog park. If your Leonberger attends puppy classes, the trainers there can recommend classes at the next level of training. Dogs of nearly any age can attend obedience training classes, although your dog should be old enough to listen to commands before instruction begins.

Obedience training usually includes the following:

- Teaching or reinforcing basic commands, like Sit, Stay, Come, and Down.
- How to walk without pulling on the leash.
- How to properly greet people and dogs, including not jumping on them.

Obedience school is as much about training you as training your dog. It helps you learn how to train your puppy while teaching your dog basic commands and how to behave for basic tasks, like greetings and walking. Classes usually last between seven and 10 weeks.

Ask your vet for recommendations, and also consider the following when evaluating trainers:

- Are they certified, particularly the CPDT-KA certification?
- How many years have they been training dogs?
- Do they have experience with training Leonbergers?
- Can you participate in the training? If the answer is no, do not use that trainer. You have to be a part of your dog's training because the trainer won't be around for most of your dog's life.

Therefore, your dog has to learn to listen to you.

If your dog has anxiety, depression, or other serious behavioral problems, you need to hire a trainer to help your dog work through those issues. Do your research to be sure your trainer is an expert—preferably one with experience training intelligent, strong-willed dogs.

Once your Leonberger understands the basic commands and has done well in obedience training, you will know if more difficult training is right for him.

CHAPTER 12
Socialization

If you adopt a puppy, you will find socialization to be one of the easiest things that you do. They do have some protective instincts after they become adults, so socialization is essential (just as much so that they aren't so excited they jump up on people). By nature, they do want to have fun, especially if everyone is feeling good.

As mentioned in an earlier chapter, males can be more aggressive toward other male dogs. Early socialization will help to make sure that potential issue is minimized early.

Another benefit of early socialization is that it can make life much more enjoyable for everyone involved, no matter what the situation. A socialized dog will approach the world from a much better place than a dog who is not socialized.

Greeting New People

Puppies will likely enjoy meeting new people, so make sure to invite friends over to help socialize your new canine family member. Your Leonberger may initially react by barking, but this likely will stop as soon as the person tries to pet your pooch. Still, you will need to be careful to make sure that there are no territorial behaviors.

The following is a list of methods to use when introducing your puppy to a new person:

- Try to have your puppy meet new people daily, if possible. This could be during walks or while you are doing other activities, both inside and outside of the house. If you can't meet new people daily, try to do so at least four times a week.

- Invite friends and family over and let them spend a few minutes giving the puppy their undivided attention. If your puppy has a favorite game or activity, let people know so they can play with him. This will win the little guy over very quickly and teach him new people are fun and safe to be around.

- Once your puppy is old enough to learn to do tricks (after the first month), have your little friend perform his tricks for visitors.

- Avoid crowds for the first few months. When your puppy is older, attend dog-friendly events so your pup can learn to be comfortable around a large group of people.

Greeting New Dogs

> *Leo puppies may be big in size, but they are typically uncoordinated and awkward. Often puppy playmates that are best suited in age are not the best suited in size. Find appropriate playmates that won't be too rough and accidentally hurt a young puppy. Always monitor playtime to avoid injuries, and ensure your puppy has adequate time to sleep after a fun social outing.*
>
> ERIN ANDERSEN
> *High Hopes Newfoundlands and Leonbergers*

HELPFUL TIP
Walking Management

Leonbergers are on the larger side of dog breeds, making pulling on the leash a particularly daunting problem. If your Leonberger is prone to pulling, managing your dog in certain situations could be more challenging. A straightforward trick for training your dog to stop pulling on the leash is introducing a head collar. These collars fasten around your dog's nose and ears and can give added control when walking a large-breed dog. A second leash should be attached to a regular harness or neck collar for added security. Introducing a head collar may take time and patience since dogs can be sensitive about wearing things around their heads.

Chapter 8 explained how to introduce your new Leonberger to your other dogs. However, meeting dogs that are not part of your household is a little different, especially since you may encounter them at any time when you are out walking. The goal is to be able to walk around your neighborhood while your dog remains calm, refraining from running up to other dogs that may not be as friendly. The problem will likely be with the other dog, particularly if the other dog is not sociable; having a dog running toward it may be upsetting. Therefore, you need to train your Leonberger as early as possible to keep him safe.

Most dogs will bow and sniff each other during an introduction. Remember to watch for signs of aggression (Chapter 8), such as raised hackles and bared teeth. It is unlikely, but it is best to be safe. Bowing, high tail, and perked ears usually mean that your Leonberger is excited about meeting the other dog. If your Leonberger is making noises, make sure that the sounds are playful by paying attention to the physical reaction. This applies more if you adopted an adult than if you have a puppy, but it is always a good idea to keep an eye out for these signs, regardless of the age of your dog.

The best way to help a Leonberger feel comfortable around unfamiliar dogs is to set up playdates with other dogs in a neutral place. This should make the whole experience much easier.

Don't let your Leonberger jump up on other dogs, no matter how excited he is. This action can become a way of showing dominance, which you really don't want with your puppy, even if it is just play in the beginning. If he does jump up, immediately say, "No," to let him know it is not acceptable behavior.

The Importance of Continuing Socialization

Even friendly dogs need socialization. When family and friends visit, encourage them to bring their dogs. This will remind your Leonberger his home is a welcoming place and not somewhere he needs to exert his dominance. You do not want your pup to think he can be a terror in his own house.

Socializing an Adult Dog

Socializing an adult canine requires a lot of time, dedication, gentle training, and a firm approach. There's no guarantee that your dog will be happy being around other dogs. You may be lucky enough to get an adult that is already well-socialized. That does not mean you can remain entirely relaxed! Your new dog may have had a terrible experience with a particular breed of dog that no one knows about, and this can result in a bad situation.

Your dog should be adept at the following commands before you work on socialization:

- Sit
- Down
- Stay
- Heel

"Heel" and "Stay" are especially important because they demonstrate that your dog has self-control by remaining in one place based on your command. This quality will be helpful when socializing because using this command will allow you to control your Leonberger in any situation. When you go outside, you will need to be very aware of your surroundings and be able to command your dog before another dog or person gets near you.

Photo Courtesy of Sandy Geldhof

- Use a short leash on walks. Being aware of your surroundings will start to cue you in to what is making your dog react, so you can start training him not to react negatively.

- Change direction if you notice your Leonberger is not reacting well to a person or dog that is

118

Photo Courtesy
of Storme Gabriel

approaching. Avoidance is a good short-term solution until you know your dog is more accepting of the presence of other dogs or people.

- If you are not able to take a different direction, tell your dog to sit, then block his view. This can prove to be particularly challenging, as he will try to look around you. Continue to distract your dog so he will listen to you, taking his mind off what is coming toward him.

- Ask friends with friendly dogs to visit you, then meet in an enclosed space. Having one or two friendly dogs to interact with can help your Leonberger realize not all dogs are dangerous or need to be put in their place. When dogs wander around the area together, with no real inter-action, your dog will learn that the others are enjoying the outside too. So, there is no reason to try to bully them!

- Get special treats for when you go walking. If your dog is aggressive when walking, have him sit and give him one of the special treats. Leonbergers are food motivated, so this could be a perfect way of distracting your dog from whatever is making him feel protective. At the first snarl or sign of aggression, engage the training mentality and draw upon your dog's desire for those special treats. This method is slow, but it is reli-able because your dog will learn that the appearance of strangers and other dogs means special treats for him. He will realize going on a walk is a positive experience, not a negative one. Nonetheless, this does not train him to interact with those dogs. Combine this tip with the previous suggestion to get the best results.

If you have ongoing problems with your adult dog, consult a behaviorist or specialized trainer.

Photo Courtesy
of Barbara Zwierzynska

CHAPTER 13

Playtime and Exercise

Leonbergers' energy level is what draws some people to them. They can keep up with you for so many activities, and you don't have to worry about moving too fast for them. This is a breed that can do pretty much anything you do and will happily join in your activities. When your active day is over, they make fantastic cuddle buddies as you relax. Conversely, when you own a Leonberger, you also really can't afford to take a day off from exercising because your dog is absolutely going to need daily activity.

Photo Courtesy of Alitza Vagenknechtova

There are a number of positives for your dog when you ensure he gets regular exercise sessions.

- It helps keep your dog at a healthier weight.
- He will be tired enough not to be too much trouble, especially if you need to leave him alone for a little while.
- Exercise is a great time to bond with your Leonberger.

Exercise Needs

Leos are active, especially in their youth. A tired dog/puppy is typically a well-behaved dog/puppy, so I encourage enough activity for both physical and mental health. Swimming is my go-to for fitness as my dogs tend to love it, and it's good for both puppies and adults. Walking and hiking are also good, and if you are working on performance titles (obedience, rally, drafting etc.), all of that work will assist in getting your Leo in shape. Leos do need daily exercise, so try to fill each day with something like a walk, playtime with another dog, an obedience class, etc.

ERIN ANDERSEN
High Hopes Newfoundlands and Leonbergers

Leonbergers need at least an hour of vigorous daily exercise until they reach their senior years (Chapter 18). Aim for a 30-minute activity in the morning and another 30-minute round of activities in the evening. On weekends and vacation days, you can spend a lot more time out of doors having fun. If your Leonberger is not getting enough activity, it will probably be very obvious. He will take out his energy and boredom on your furniture, doors, and home.

Leonbergers aren't the best breed for jogging. They can keep up, but high-impact exercises can hurt their joints. Also, they are more likely to overheat. It is best to do lower-impact activities for longer periods of time.

You will definitely have your limits about how much cold and rainy weather you can handle. This doesn't mean that your Leonberger can skip being active—not if you don't want your dog to take it out around your home. Fortunately, there are plenty of indoor activities that you can do on days when going outside really isn't such a good idea.

Outdoor Activities

> *My Leos love to go on walks or hikes! We live in a pretty warm climate, so in the warmer months, we do a lot of swimming, which they LOVE! I also think it's great to do classes with your dog. Try agility, barn hunts, trick classes. Just like people, Leos can get bored doing the same thing all the time, so try to keep things interesting, even if it's just walking on different streets or going to different parks!*
>
> ELLIE ADAMS
> *Rocky Ford Leonbergers*

The possibilities are pretty much endless in terms of what your Leonberger can do outside. If you live in an area with snow, he will be the perfect companion for kids playing in the snow or going out to do chores and other activities in the cold.

An Avid Swimmer

Don't be fooled into thinking that a Leonberger's thick double coat is a problem for the dog in the water—that thick coat is waterproof. Also, they have webbed feet. This is a dog that can keep up with you in the pool or a natural body of water—though admittedly, your pool filter may not be capable of handling all the fur your dog sheds during a swim.

Start your Leonberger in pools, ponds, and smaller lakes. Shallower depths can help your dog feel safer faster. Don't worry—you don't have to teach your dog to swim. Any initial apprehension will give way to those well-honed instincts, and your dog will be swimming much faster than any human, usually by the end of the first swim. Still, keep going to the shallower locations for at least the first few swims.

Once your dog is happy and excited about water, you can move on to deeper water. Just make sure that you stay close and always keep an eye on your dog. Your Leonberger may overdo swimming in the beginning, then not have enough energy to return. If you go to an ocean or other large body of water, consider a life vest for your dog but also remain vigilant.

Photo Courtesy
of Lee Hickenbottom

Sledding

Sledding is only for adult Leonbergers. You need to establish a strong bond with your dog before trying this because he has to be able to listen to your commands.

To start, let your Leonberger walk around in a harness to get used to the way it feels. When the weight of the harness doesn't seem to be an issue, go through all of the training basics, particularly obedience training. If he listens to you, you can add the sled and let your dog get a feel for the additional pull and weight. It won't be long after that when you can hop on the back and enjoy a great time bonding with your dog.

Keep in mind that there should only be one person on the sled at a time; dog sledding is usually for sleighs pulled by more than one dog. Leonbergers weren't really trained to be sled dogs, so don't try to make a team pull a sleigh, as that can be disastrous. Still, it can be a great time for your dog, as long as you remember to stop this activity as your dog nears his golden years.

Dog Carting

This is an activity almost exclusively for large, sturdy dogs like the Leonberger, so it is not something most people are even aware is an option. It is very similar to horse carting but with a large dog. Leonbergers can pull several children and even an adult in a cart.

Make sure you begin helping your dog get accustomed to pulling the cart with nothing inside it. Leonbergers require some time to get accustomed to the equipment and weight. Every dog will have his own comfort zone, but after a few empty carting outings, you can start letting small children onboard. Remember to make sure that the sides are sturdy and safe for the kids. Give the dog a set destination and let him get used to the weight. After a number of runs, you can try it with an adult, keeping in mind the weight and size of your dog and not putting undue stress on him by having too much weight in the cart. Don't forget that the cart also has a weight that should be included in the estimate to make sure your dog can handle it.

Hiking and Backpacking

If you love being out in nature, this is a great dog for hiking and back-packing. Leonbergers can easily keep up with you, and they will enjoy the sights as much as you (and the smells a lot more). They are the kind of dog made for being out and getting time in the woods, mountains, and forests, making them the ideal companion for outdoor enthusiasts.

Advanced Training

Though they are big, Leonbergers are incredibly agile, so they can play a wide range of sports, like tracking, flyball, and water sports. All of these require additional training specific to the sports, but if you find you want to branch out beyond the other activities, the possibilities for a large, energetic, intelligent breed like the Leonberger are pretty much endless.

You can even have your Leonberger join a water rescue. The training is rigorous, but it is an activity at which this breed tends to excel.

*Photo Courtesy
of Caitlin MacFarlane*

Indoor Activities

> **"**
>
> *Mental stimulation can be just as exhausting for puppies as physical stimulation. I encourage short training sessions multiple times per day, especially if you're unable to be physically active due to weather, etc. Leos are very smart and love to learn.*
>
> ERIN ANDERSEN
> *High Hopes Newfoundlands and Leonbergers*
>
> **"**

The real downside to larger dogs is that during bad weather, it is much harder to make sure they get their daily exercise.

Hide and Seek

Hide and seek is a game you can play once your dog understands proper behavior in the home. Since your Leonberger will probably hear you wherever you hide, you can also make it a game of hide the toy. If you distract your pup while someone else hides the toy, your Leonberger will have a fun time trying to locate it!

More Training

Rollover, play dead, and pretty much anything else you want to teach your dog are activities you can do on gloomy or hot days so that he is tired at the end of the day.

Puzzle Toys!

Puzzle toys are a fun way to get your dog to move around without you having to do much. Most puzzle toys are food-based, so the dog will need to figure out how to get the treats out. If you use these toys, keep in mind that your dog isn't likely to work off the extra calories consumed from puzzle treats, and you should adjust his meals accordingly.

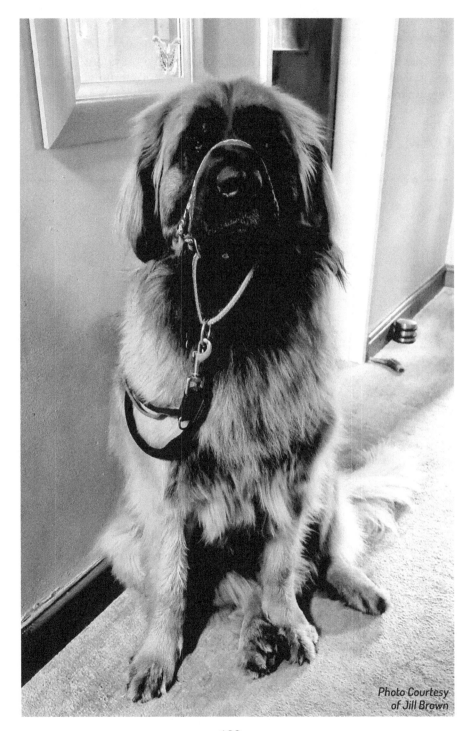

Photo Courtesy of Jill Brown

What to Avoid

There are a lot of things you can do to exercise a Leonberger, but with an intelligent dog like this, you have to be very careful about not letting him get into trouble. The following are things you should avoid.

Overexertion in Puppies

> *Leos are fast-growing dogs. They need a lot of exercise to help them grow muscle mass. However, don't be surprised if your Leo has growing pains. This is normal, especially in tall males. Your dog may experience leg pain and may even limp. Shorter periods of low-impact exercise will help, like walking in sand or up small hills.*
>
> PAULA DEVORE
> *Rev It Up Kennel*

Leonberger puppies grow rapidly, meaning their growth plates are not closed until the dog is about 18 months old. The best way to work out the energy of a Leonberger puppy is to give him a lot of off-leash play on soft surfaces, such as lawns. Swimming is also a great activity since this is a breed that takes to water like a duck, and it won't hurt their joints.

Puppies are also tired as much by mental work as by physical activity. They don't require nearly as much activity to tire as an adult. Let their flagging energy levels help you determine when to stop play, and be ready for them to be energetic all too soon afterward.

FUN FACT
Dock Jumping

Leonbergers are strong swimmers, equipped with webbed feet, which help them swim more efficiently. These dogs can be excellent water rescue animals who may enjoy the exercise and entertainment of dock jumping. Dock jumping or dock diving is a sport where dogs compete for height and distance when jumping from a dock into the water. Leos typically love water, making dock jumping an excellent way to burn off energy, as well as compete with other dogs.

Hot Weather

Chapter 15 details best grooming practices for this breed, but hot weather is always going to be problematic for Leonbergers. Avoid exercising during the heat of the day. If a dog gets too hot, he can suffer heat stress, or in worst cases, heatstroke. The following are signs that your dog may be suffering from one of these conditions:

- Excessive panting or whining

- Sudden lethargy or confusion

- Tongue is hanging out more than usual and is shaped like a scoop at the end

- Gums and tongue appear red

Photo Courtesy Barbara Zwierzynska

It is best to keep your Leonberger inside on hot days and do the indoor activities. If you do want to go outside to be active, do it either very early in the morning or around/after dusk.

Post Meal Exercise

Unfortunately, Leonbergers are at risk of gastric dilation volvulus, better known as bloat. The ailment is covered in detail in Chapter 17, but one of the ways to increase the risk of this life-threatening problem is to exercise your dog right after eating. Give your dog at least an hour to digest his food before you do any kind of exercising; some experts recommend waiting two hours to be safe.

PART 4

TAKING CARE OF YOUR LEONBERGER

CHAPTER 14
Nutrition

All large dogs require a considerable amount of attention to their diet to ensure that they remain healthy, have a high quality of life, and live as long as possible. Considering puppies are typically full-grown at about one year but are not considered to be adults until they are around three, it is essential to ensure your high-energy puppy has the right foods to help him grow strong and healthy.

Why a Healthy Diet is Important

Just because your Leonberger is active doesn't mean he is burning all the calories he takes in, especially if you have an open treat policy. Just as you should not be eating all day, your puppy shouldn't be either. If you have a busy schedule, it will be too easy for your dog to have substantial lapses in activity levels while you are not ensuring he gets the recommended daily exercise (covered in Chapter 14).

You need to be aware of roughly how many calories your dog eats a day, including treats, so be mindful of your dog's weight and whether or not he is putting on pounds. This will tell you if you should adjust his food intake or if you should change the food to something more nutritious but with fewer calories.

Always talk with your vet if you have concerns about your Leonberger's weight.

Dangerous Foods

Dogs can eat some raw meat without having to worry about the kinds of problems a person would encounter because they are able to eat a number of animals raw. However, there are some human foods that could be fatal to your Leonberger, in part because the kinds of raw meat that humans offer have been farmed and treated with a range of chemicals and other unnatural treatments to boost their size. Raw diets will be examined later in this chapter so you can protect your Leonberger from the potential risks associated with raw foods.

The following is a list of foods you should NEVER feed your dog:

- Apple seeds
- Chocolate
- Coffee
- Cooked bones (They can kill a dog when the bones splinter in the dog's mouth or stomach.)
- Corn on the cob (The cob is deadly to dogs; corn off the cob is fine.)
- Grapes/raisins
- Macadamia nuts
- Onions and chives
- Peaches, persimmons, and plums
- Tobacco (Your Leonberger will not realize it is not a food and may eat it if it's left out.)
- Xylitol (a sugar substitute in candies and baked goods)
- Yeast

In addition to this list, consult the Canine Journal for a lengthy list of other dangerous foods. (http://www.caninejournal.com/foods-not-to-feed-dog/)

Canine Nutrition

Canines are largely carnivorous, and protein is a significant dietary need (as discussed later in this chapter). However, they need more than just protein to be healthy.

The following table provides the primary nutritional requirements for dogs:

Nutrient	Sources	Puppy	Adult
Protein	meat, eggs, soybeans, corn, wheat, peanut butter	22.0% of diet	18.0% of diet
Fats	fish oil, flaxseed oil, canola oil, pork fat, poultry fat, safflower oil, sunflower oil, soybean oil	8.0 to 15.0% of diet	5.0 to 15.0% of diet
Calcium	dairy, animal organ tissue, meats, legumes (typically beans)	1.0% of diet	0.6% of diet
Phosphorus	meat and pet supplements	0.8% of diet	0.5% of diet
Sodium	meat, eggs	0.3% of diet	0.06% of diet

The following are the remaining nutrients dogs require, all of them less than 1% of a puppy or an adult diet:

- Arginine
- Histidine
- Isoleucine
- Leucine
- Lysine
- Methionine + cystine
- Phenylalanine + tyrosine
- Threonine
- Tryptophan
- Valine
- Chloride

It is best to avoid giving your dog human foods with a lot of sodium and preservatives. Water is also absolutely essential to keep your dog healthy. Make a habit of checking your dog's water bowl several times a day so that your dog does not get dehydrated.

Proteins and Amino Acids

Since dogs are carnivores, protein is one of the most important nutrients in a healthy dog's diet. (Dogs should not eat as much meat as their close wolf relatives do. Dogs' diets and needs have changed significantly since they have become human companions.) Proteins contain the necessary amino acids for your dog to produce glucose, which is essential for giving your dog energy. A lack of protein in your dog's diet will result in him being lethargic. His coat may start to look dull, and he is likely to lose weight. Conversely, if your dog gets too much protein, his body will store the excess protein as fat, and he will gain weight.

Meat is the best source of protein for your dog, and a dog's dietary needs are significantly different from a human's needs. If you plan to feed your dog a vegetarian diet, it is very important that you talk to your vet first. It is incredibly difficult to ensure that a carnivore receives adequate protein while on a vegetarian diet. Puppies, in particular, need to have adequate protein to be healthy adults, so you may need to give your puppy a diet with meat, then switch to a vegetarian diet after your Leonberger becomes an adult.

Protein is particularly important for taking care of your Leonberger's coat. While you don't want to be excessive, do make sure that your dog gets adequate protein every day. This will be easier if you make meals for your dog. If you don't have time, make sure to buy foods that are high in protein.

Fat and Fatty Acids

Most fats that your dog needs are found in meat. Seed oils provide a lot of necessary healthy fats, too, with peanut butter being one of the most common sources. Fats break down into fatty acids, which your dog needs for fat-soluble vitamins that help with regular cell functions. Perhaps the most obvious benefit of fats and fatty acids can be seen in your dog's coat. Your Leonberger's coat will look and feel much healthier when he is getting the right nutrients.

The following is a list of potential health issues that might arise if your dog does not get adequate fats in his daily diet:

- His coat will look less healthy.
- His skin may be dry and itchy.
- His immune system could be compromised, making it easier for your dog to get sick.
- He may have an increased risk of heart disease. The primary concern if your dog gets too much fat is that he will become obese, leading to additional health problems.

Carbohydrates and Cooked Foods

Dogs have been living with humans for millennia, so their dietary needs have evolved like our own. They can eat foods with carbohydrates to supplement the energy typically provided by proteins and fats. If you cook grains (such as barley, corn, and rice) prior to feeding them to your dog, it will be easier for him to digest those complex carbohydrates. If your dog is allergic to grains, potatoes and sweet potatoes are also high in carbohydrates.

Different Dietary Requirements for Different Life Stages

Different stages of a dog's life have different nutritional needs.

Puppy Food

During roughly the first 12 months of their lives, puppies' bodies are growing. Their nutritional needs are much different from their adult counterparts. To be healthy, they need more calories and have different nutritional needs to promote growth, so feed them a food made specifically for puppies. Puppies can have up to four meals a day. Just be careful not to overfeed them, particularly if you use treats during training.

Adult Dog Food

The primary difference between puppy food and adult dog food is puppy food is higher in calories and nutrients. Dog food manufacturers reduce these nutrients in adult dog food, as they no longer need lots of calories to sustain growth. As a rule, when a canine reaches about 90% of his predicted adult size, you should switch to adult dog food.

The size of your Leonberger is key in determining how much to feed him. The following table is a general recommendation for your adult Leonberger's daily food consumption. Initially, you may want to focus on the calories as you try to find the right balance for your dog.

Dog Size	Calories per day
70 – 100 lbs	1,680 during hot months 2,500 during cold months
100 + lbs	2,400 during hot months 3,600 during cold months

To minimize the risk of bloat (covered in Chapter 17), you should feed your Leonberger at least twice a day (rather than feeding him just one big meal), so you can divide up the calories according to this schedule. Keep in mind these recommendations are per day and not per meal. To make sure your dog feels like a real part of the family, let your pup eat when you do, even if he doesn't get that much food at a time.

It is also recommended that you set the food and water bowls at an elevated level so that your dog doesn't have to lean over so far to eat. This can help reduce the risk of bloat as well. If you notice your Leonberger eating too quickly, consider a dog feeder that limits how quickly he can eat. After 15 minutes, pick up the food bowl so that he does not continuously eat over the course of the day. However, always leave fresh water out for your dog, making it easily accessible all day and night.

If you plan to add wet food, pay attention to the total calorie

FUN FACT
Guinness Record Holder

A Leonberger named Hagrid holds the Guinness World Record for "most items caught by a dog in 30 seconds." Weighing in at 154 pounds, Hagrid drew a crowd at the National Pet Show in Birmingham, where he caught and ate 13 sausages in 30 seconds.

intake, and adjust how much you feed your dog between the kibble and wet food. The total calories in the kibble and wet food should balance out so as not to exceed your dog's needs. The same is true if you give your dog a lot of treats over the course of the day. You should factor treat calories into how much you feed your dog at mealtimes.

If you feed your dog homemade food (discussed later in this chapter), you should learn your nutrition facts, and you should pay close attention to calories instead of cup measurements.

Senior Dog Food

Senior dogs are not always capable of being as active as they were in their younger days. If you notice your dog is slowing down or suffers joint pain and shows a lack of stamina when taking long walks, you can assume your Leonberger is entering his senior years. Consult with your vet if you think it is time to change the type of food you feed your dog.

The primary difference between adult and senior dog food is senior dog food contains less fat and more antioxidants to help fight weight gain. Senior dogs also need more protein, which will probably make your dog happy because that usually means more meat. Protein helps to maintain your dog's aging muscles. He should also be eating less phosphorus during his golden years to avoid the risk of developing hyperphosphatemia. This is a condition where dogs have excessive amounts of phosphorus in their bloodstream, and older dogs are at greater risk of developing it. The level of phosphorus in the body is controlled by the kidneys; as such, elevated levels of phosphorus are usually an indication of a problem with the kidneys.

Senior dog food has the correct number of calories for reduced activity, which means no adjustment of quantity is needed unless you notice weight gain. Consult your vet if you notice your dog is putting on weight because this could be a sign of illness.

Your Dog's Meal Options

You have three primary choices for what to feed your dog, or you can use a combination of the three, depending on your situation and your dog's specific needs.

Commercial Food

Make sure that you are buying the best dog food you can afford. Take the time to research each of your options, particularly the nutritional value of the food, and review this annually. Make sure the food you are giving your dog is high quality, and always take into account your dog's size, energy level, and age. Your puppy may not need puppy food for as long as other breeds, and dog food for seniors may not be necessary for Leonbergers. You'll need to pay attention to your dog's individual needs to determine if he needs a special food for his age.

The website *Pawster* provides several great articles about which commercial dog foods are best for Leonbergers. Since new foods frequently come on the market, check periodically to see if there are new, better foods that have become available.

If you aren't sure which brand of food is best, talk with the breeder about the foods they recommend. Breeders are really the best guides for you here, as they are experts, but you can also ask your vet.

Some dogs may be picky eaters that get tired of repeatedly eating the same food. While you shouldn't frequently change the brand of food because that can upset your dog's stomach, you can get foods that have assorted flavors. You can also change the taste by adding a bit of wet (canned) food.

Dry Dog Food

PROS

- Convenience
- Variety
- Availability
- Affordability
- Manufacturers follow nutritional recommendations (not all of them follow this, so do your brand research before you buy)
- Specially formulated for different canine life stages
- Can be used for training
- Easy to store

CONS

- Requires research to ensure you don't buy doggie junk food
- Packaging is not always honest
- Recalls for food contamination
- Loose FDA nutritional regulations
- Low quality food may have questionable ingredients

Adding one-fourth to one-third of a can for each meal is an easy change to make to ensure your dog's happiness.

For more details on commercial options, check out the website Dog Food Advisor. They provide reviews on various dog food brands, as well as providing information on recalls and contamination issues.

COMMERCIAL DRY FOOD

Dry dog food often comes in bags, and it is what the vast majority of people feed their dogs.

The convenience and ease on your budget mean you are almost certainly going to buy kibble for your dog. This is perfectly fine, and most dogs will be more than happy to eat kibble. Be sure you know what brand you are feeding your dog, and pay attention to kibble recalls so you can stop feeding your dog a certain brand if necessary. Check out the following sites regularly for recall information:

- Dog Food Recalls – www.dogfoodadvisor.com
- American Kennel Club – www.AKC.org
- Dog Food Guide – www.dogfood.guide

Wet Dog Food

PROS	CONS
• Helps keep dogs hydrated	• Dog bowls must be washed after every meal
• Has a richer scent and flavor	• Can soften bowel movements
• Easier to eat for dogs with dental problems (particularly those missing teeth) or if a dog has been ill	• Can be messier than kibble
• Convenient and easy to serve	• Once opened, it has a very short shelf life, and should be covered and refrigerated
• Unopened, it can last between 1 and 3 years	• More expensive than dry dog food, and comes in small quantities
• Balanced based on current pet nutrition recommendations	• Packaging is not always honest
	• Recalls for food contamination
	• Loose FDA regulations

COMMERCIAL WET FOOD

Most dogs prefer wet dog food over kibble, but it is also more expensive. Wet dog food can be purchased in large packs that can be extremely easy to store.

Like dry dog food, wet dog food is convenient, and picky dogs are much more likely to eat it than kibble. If your dog gets sick, use wet dog food to ensure that he is still eating and gets the necessary nutrition each day. It may be harder to switch back to kibble once your Leonberger is healthy, but you can always add a little wet food to make each meal more appetizing.

Raw Diet

For dogs prone to food allergies, raw diets can help prevent an allergic reaction to wheat and processed foods. Raw diets are heavy in raw meats, bones, vegetables, and specific supplements. Some of the benefits of a raw diet include:

- Improves your dog's coat and skin
- Improves immune system
- Improves health (as a result of better digestion)
- Increases energy
- Increases muscle mass

Raw diets are meant to give your dog the kind of food canines ate before being domesticated. It means giving your dog uncooked meats, whole (uncooked) bones, and a small amount of dairy products. It doesn't include processed food of any kind—not even food cooked in your kitchen.

There are potential risks to this diet. Dogs have been domesticated for millennia, and their digestive systems have also evolved. Trying to force them to eat the kind of diet they ate hundreds of years ago does not always work as intended, primarily because dogs may not be able to fully digest raw food the way their ancestors did. Part of the problem is that the kinds of raw meat we have at home aren't wild, with many farmed animals having chemicals, hormones, and other treatments that are not natural. Also, dogs' digestive systems have been evolving so that some of them are not able to fully process raw meat the way canines 200 years ago did.

There are also many risks associated with feeding dogs uncooked meals, particularly if the food has been contaminated. Things like bacteria pose a serious risk and can be transferred to you if your dog gets sick. Many medical professionals also warn about the dangers of giving dogs bones even if they are uncooked. Bones can splinter in your dog's mouth and puncture the esophagus or stomach.

The Canine Journal (www.caninejournal.com) provides a lot of information about a raw diet, including different recipes and how to transition your dog to this diet. Always talk to your veterinarian before putting your dog on a new kind of diet.

Homemade Diet

The best home-cooked meals should be planned in advance so that your Leonberger gets the correct nutritional balance. Typically, 50% of your dog's food should be animal protein (fish, poultry, and organ meats). About 25% should be full of complex carbohydrates. The remaining 25% should be from fruits and vegetables, particularly foods like pumpkin, apples, bananas, and green beans. These foods provide extra flavor your Leonberger will probably love while filling him up faster and reducing the chance of overeating.

The following are a few sites where you can learn how to make homemade meals for canines. Most of them are not breed-specific, so if you have more than one dog, these meals can be made for all your furry canine friends:

- Cairn Talk: Homemade Food (https://www.cairntalk.net/topic/15382-homemade-food/)
- Holistic Diet for Leonbergers (https://pets.thenest.com/holistic-diet-cairn-terriers-6665.html)
- Easy Homemade Dog Food Recipe (https://thismessisours.com/easy-homemade-dog-food-recipe/)
- Tasty Low Carb (https://www.tasty-lowcarb.com/healthy-homemade-dog-food/)
- Hublore (http://hublore.blogspot.com/2011/05/homemade-dog-food-recipe.html)
- Homemade Dog Food with a Special Ingredient (https://pethelpful.com/dogs/Homemade-Dog-Food-with-an-Extra-Special-Ingredient)
- Canine Journal (https://www.caninejournal.com/homemade-dog-food-recipes/)
- DIY Homemade Dog Food (https://damndelicious.net/2015/04/27/diy-homemade-dog-food/)

Keep in mind the foods your Leonberger absolutely should not eat. You can also mix some of the food you make for yourself into your Leonberger's meal.

Do not feed your Leonberger from your plate! Split the food, placing your dog's meal into a bowl so that your canine understands your food is just for you.

Scheduling Meals

Your Leonberger will probably expect you to stick to a schedule, which definitely includes mealtimes. If treats and snacks are something you establish as a normal routine, your dog will expect that too! For puppies, plan to have three or four meals, while adults and seniors should typically have two meals a day.

Food Allergies and Intolerance

Whenever you start your dog on a new type of food (even if it's simply a different flavor), you need to monitor him while he becomes accustomed to the change. Food allergies are fairly common in Leonbergers, and the symptoms manifest themselves as hot spots, which are similar to rashes in humans. Your dog may start scratching or chewing specific spots on his body, and his fur or hair could start falling out around those spots. Some dogs don't have individual hot spots, but the allergy shows up on their entire coat. If your Leonberger seems to be shedding more hair than normal, take him to the vet to be checked for food allergies.

If you give your dog something his stomach cannot handle, it will probably be obvious when your dog is unable to hold his bowels. If he is already house-trained, he will probably either pant at you or whimper to let you know he needs to go outside. Get him outside as quickly as you can so that he does not have an accident. Flatulence will also probably occur more often if your Leonberger has a food intolerance.

Since the symptoms of food allergies and intolerances look similar to a reaction to nutritional deficiencies, you should visit your vet immediately! This is especially true if you notice any problems with your dog's coat or skin.

Photo Courtesy of Barbara Zwierzynska

CHAPTER 15
Grooming – Productive Bonding

As you likely already suspect, that gorgeous Leonberger coat is actually pretty high maintenance, not in terms of supplies, but in terms of time. There is a lot of dog to groom, and you are going to need to check for tangles and mats at least several times a week. Taking your Leonberger outside to play in the grass, woods, or other locations often results in his fur getting leaves and debris in it. Considering how active the breed can be, planning for daily brushings is probably the best way to go—you won't get a break in the colder months as this is when Leonbergers really enjoy being outside. Then again, grooming your Leonberger after being outside is not only a way to bond; in the colder times of the year, it gives you a way to warm up by brushing all of your dog's thick fur!

HELPFUL TIP
Big Dog, Big Brush

Leonbergers' large stature comes with a large amount of fluffy fur. Their double coat keeps them warm in winter but can become tangled without regular grooming. When looking for a brush, be sure to purchase one with bristles that are long enough to penetrate through the thick fur and reach the fur closest to your dog's skin, as this is where mats can go undetected and become unmanageable. Pin brushes are a good candidate for this. In addition, slicker brushes, de-shedding brushes, and grooming combs are great tools to keep in your grooming arsenal.

You will need to groom both the top coat and the undercoat to ensure that the dog doesn't have tangles or mats. Baths happen about every six to eight weeks, which can make it very interesting as this is a big dog that may not be as fond of water in the tub as it is with being in the water outside. You will almost certainly need to trim your dog's fur, especially around the paws, which is why some experts recommend taking your Leonberger to a professional groomer in the early days to learn how to do this properly.

Then, there are the other regular grooming tasks, such as brushing your dog's teeth and trimming his nails. You will need to budget for professional help with your dog's paws and nails, as Leonberger paws and nails are far more complicated than most other breeds. This will be covered in a bit more detail later in the chapter.

Photo Courtesy
of Ashley Cote

Grooming Focus and Tools

> **"**
>
> *As with any double-coated breed, weekly combing is essential. Mats tend to creep in daily in the ear and backside. I prefer using a greyhound comb for all of my grooming, but if there's a huge mess, I will start with a long-toothed slicker brush. If bathing, ensure your dog gets completely dry or hot spots may result. Start with nails (I prefer a Dremel) when your dog is a puppy so that it is easy to keep them short. Leos like to paw people, and nothing is worse than long nails that scratch someone's arms or legs.*
>
> ERIN ANDERSEN
> *High Hopes Newfoundlands and Leonbergers*
>
> **"**

Given how often Leonbergers need to be groomed, it probably comes as a relief that you can easily take care of most of it at home. There are still a few things that we strongly recommend seeing an expert about in the early days to learn how to take care of your Leonberger (all paw related), but for the most part, you should be able to take care of your dog yourself. This is not a breed for new dog families, especially because there is a lot more to do for that coat, so it will take time, energy, and patience. Fortunately, Leonbergers are known for being very patient, so except for the puppy years, your dog will likely not give you trouble as you try to take care of that luxurious coat. In fact, he'll probably be pleased for the dedicated time and attention. It is also healthier for the dog if you do most of the grooming, as there are some issues that you are more likely to notice if you groom him several times a week (see Chapters 16 and 17).

Leonbergers have an outercoat and an undercoat, both of which can mat and retain debris. You have two primary purposes for those regular brushings:

1. Remove mats from both coats, which means regularly brushing to keep large mats from forming. This includes brushing around your Leonberger's head and behind the ears, around the legs and tail, and along the large chest—these are the areas where mats tend to form. If a large mat does form, it is better to trim the mat than to try to brush it out. Small mats and tangles are removed with mat combs and slicker brushes.

*Photo Courtesy
of Barbara Zwierzynska*

2. Remove the extra hair from the undercoat; this is a task that can be significantly sped up if you have a high-velocity dryer or other quick method of removing the excess hair. You can also brush the undercoat by hand, but it will take a lot longer than using a tool designed to remove the fur. Either way, it can get really messy because there will seem to be an endless supply of hair that needs to be removed.

Here's a quick summary of the best tools to take care of your Leonberger's coat:

- Grooming comb for removing mats
- A slicker brush to gently spread your dog's natural oils over his body
- Small scissors to remove mats
- High-velocity dryer or undercoat rake
- Stripping knives, which are made based on a person's dominant hand; they help remove extra undercoat fur
- Shampoo (Make sure you use dog shampoo, not human, and check Bark Space for the latest recommendations.)
- Nail trimmers
- Toothbrush and dog toothpaste (not human—it's toxic for dogs!). (Check the American Kennel Club for the latest recommendations for the Leonberger, as they tend to have dental problems.)

Coat Management

Brush EVERY DAY. If you do it every day, it takes less than five minutes and helps avoid mats forming. I teach my dogs to stand with their front feet in a chair outside (on a low, large chair). That way, I can easily brush up and down each side. (Ears and 'breeches' tend to be problem areas). I start this with my Leos when they are young, so they grow up knowing that is just what we do after breakfast! Makes it quick and easy!

ELLIE ADAMS
Rocky Ford Leonbergers

Always make sure to tire your dog before you start brushing. You cannot rush the process. To get all of the tangles and other issues taken care of, you are going to need a good bit of time, so you need your dog to sit still for a while. You'll know when you don't need to dedicate time to tiring your dog when he starts to slow down as a senior or shows an interest in just sitting and letting you pet and brush him.

For all ages, if the mats are severe, it is recommended to cut them off instead of trying to brush them out—given their fur, it is much more humane to simply cut a mat than to drag out the removal process. You will want to start with a coarse brush and remove tangles carefully as you go. After the tangles and small mats are removed, change to a slicker brush to spread the natural oils from the skin through the coat. Always brush your dog's hair before you attempt to roll his coat so that tangles are removed, making the rolling much easier.

Puppies

The difficulty when grooming a puppy is fairly universal because puppies are notorious for squirming! A daily brushing is the best way to prevent matted hair and to bond with your dog. Yes, it will be a bit challenging in the beginning because puppies don't sit still for prolonged periods of time; there will be a lot of wiggling and attempts to play. Trying to tell your puppy that the brush is not a toy clearly won't work, so be patient during each brushing session!

On the other hand, your pup will be so adorable that you probably won't mind a grooming session taking a bit longer than expected. Just make sure you let your pup know grooming is serious business, and playing comes after grooming. Otherwise, your Leonberger is going to always try to play, which will make brushing him even more time-consuming.

Try planning to brush your puppy after a vigorous exercise session. If you find your puppy has trouble sitting still, you can make brushing sessions shorter, but do it more than once a day until he gets used to the routine.

Adult Dogs

Brushing needs to be done several times a week for the adults, especially after a lot of outdoor activity. Remember to start with the coarse brush to remove the tangles and smooth the hair, and then move to the slicker brush. The grooming process stimulates the skin to release oils that make the fur shinier and more resistant to dirt, and this is absolutely necessary for Leonbergers. If you regularly brush your dog, it can help reduce how often you have to bathe him.

Brushing your dog is about more than just removing excess fur and improving the coat's shine. You need to spend each grooming session looking for skin problems, lumps, flea or tick bites, and other problems when you brush your buddy. This will reveal any potential issues that you should monitor and follow up with a trip to the vet if symptoms become severe.

If you rescued an adult Leonberger, it might take a little while to get the dog used to being brushed frequently. If your dog does not feel comfortable in the beginning when you brush his fur, work the routine into your schedule, just like training, so he will get accustomed to the task.

Senior Dogs

You can brush your senior dog more often if you would like, as the extra affection and time you give him will likely be welcome. You will probably find there are fewer tangles and small mats as your dog slows down, but the grooming process can be incredibly welcome in older Leonbergers. After all, he's slowing down, and just relaxing with you will be enjoyable for him (and the warmth of your hands will feel really good on his aging body). Grooming sessions are an appropriate time to check for problems while giving your older pup a nice massage to ease any pain. Look for any changes to the skin, such as bumps or fatty lumps. These may need to be mentioned to the vet during a regular visit.

Allergies

Many Leonbergers have skin allergies, so keep an eye out for hot spots, or if you notice your dog's coat is thinning, then you should look for the following allergic reactions:

- Wounds take longer to heal
- Weak immune system
- Aching joints
- Hair is falling out
- Ear infections

Regular brushing keeps you aware of the health of your Leonberger's coat. This will help you identify when your big dear is suffering from allergies so that you can take him to the vet immediately.

Bath Time

Baths are recommended roughly every six to eight weeks. If your Leonberger gets muddy or really dirty, make sure to bathe him so that the dirt and mud don't get trapped in the fur or create worse problems. Avoid bathing him too often, though, since it can irritate your dog's skin and remove necessary oils in his fur. There's definitely a fine balance to bathing Leonbergers because they require bathing more often than a lot of other dogs, but it is very easy to over bathe them, thinking that it will help keep them clean (when it will actually reduce their natural oils).

Make sure the water isn't too cold or too hot but comfortably warm, and always avoid getting your dog's head wet. How to wash your dog's face is covered in the next section.

1. Gather everything you will need before you start your dog's bath. At a minimum, you need the following:

    a. shampoo and conditioners made specifically for dogs,

    b. cup for pouring water (if bathing in a tub),

    c. towels,

    d. brushes for after the drying process,

    e. nonslip tub mat if you use a tub, and

    f. buckets and a hose to rinse off if you bathe your dog outside.

2. Take your Leonberger out for a walk. This will tire your dog and make him a little hotter and less fearful—he might even appreciate the bath's cooling effect.

3. Run the water, making sure the temperature is lukewarm and not hot, especially if you have just finished a walk. If you are washing your Leonberger in a bathtub, you only need enough water to cover your pup's stomach. Do not fully cover your dog's body.

4. Pick up your dog if you are using a bathtub, and talk in a strong, confident voice.

5. Place the dog in the tub and use the cup to wash the dog. Don't use too much soap—it isn't necessary. You can fully soak the dog, starting at the neck and going to the rump. It is fine to get him wet and suds him up all at once, or you can do it a little at a time if your dog is very wiggly. Just make sure you don't get any water on his head.

6. Confidently talk to your Leonberger while you are bathing him.

7. Make sure you don't pour water on your dog's head or in his eyes or ears. Use a wet hand and gently scrub. (Follow the steps in the next section for how to carefully wash your dog's face and ears.)

Photo Courtesy of Storme Gabriel

8. When you rinse, make sure to brush up against the fur so that there is no shampoo left.

9. Take your Leonberger out of the water and towel him dry.

10. Make sure to give special attention to drying around the head and face.

11. Brush your dog when you are finished.

12. Give him a treat if he was particularly upset about the bath.

You can use these practices with other kinds of bathing, such as outside or at a public washing facility; modify them as necessary.

The first few times you bathe your dog, pay attention to the things that bother or scare your Leonberger. If he is afraid of running water, make sure you don't have the water running when your dog is in the tub. If he moves around a lot when you start to apply the shampoo, it could indicate the smell is too strong. Modify the process as necessary in order to make it as comfortable for your dog as possible.

Keep a calm, loving tone as you wash your dog to make the process a little easier next time. Sure, your Leonberger may whine, throw a tantrum, or wiggle excessively, but a calm reaction will teach your dog that bathing is a necessary part of being a member of the pack.

Cleaning Eyes and Ears

When bathing your dog, use a washcloth to wash his face and ears, and ALWAYS avoid getting water in his ears, which can lead to problems.

You will need to make weekly checks around your Leonberger's eyes and ears to detect infections early. The following are signs of a problem:

- Frequent head shaking or tilting
- Regular scratching at ears
- Swollen or red ears
- A smell or discharge from the ears

If you notice any problems with your Leonberger's ears, make an appointment with your vet. Never try to treat an infection on your own; hydrogen peroxide, cotton swabs, and other cleaning tools should never be used in a dog's ears. Your vet can show you how to clean your dog's ears correctly.

Leonbergers have a few genetic eye and ear conditions (See Chapter 17), so take time to always check your dog's eyes while you are grooming him.

Cataracts are a fairly common problem for all dogs as they age. If you see cloudy eyes, have your Leonberger checked.

After a good bath, you should take the time to trim the hair around the face and ears. This can help keep your dog's eyes and ears healthier and allow your dog to see and hear better after the cleaning.

Trimming Nails

If you have never cut a dog's nails before, do NOT start with a Leonberger. Schedule an appointment with a professional groomer who has worked with large dogs with a lot of fur. There is a lot more work to do than just trimming the nails, and NO novice should ever attempt this grooming activity without a lot of guidance and help. A professional can show you what needs to be done to trim the fur, then how to trim the nails. It is far harder to do with large dogs than with small dogs; it is almost impossible with a dog that has this much fur around the nails, in addition to having dark nails that are thicker and harder to trim.

Even if you have experience with trimming a dog's nails, it is best to seek help from a professional, as the hair around the paws will need to be trimmed and managed before the cutting can begin.

Your professional can tell you what you need to know and let you know how often your dog needs his nails trimmed based on how quickly you help wear down the nails. If you and your Leonberger spend a lot of time walking on sidewalks and concrete, it will slow the nail growth compared to regular jaunts in woods and dirt paths.

Oral Health

Leonbergers aren't prone to dental issues, but that doesn't mean that you should skip brushing your dog's teeth. Besides healthy food, there are two recommendations for taking care of your Leonberger's teeth.

1. Brush your Leonberger's teeth at least once a week.
2. Give your Leonberger dental chew treats.

Brushing Your Dog's Teeth

You have to learn to be patient and keep teeth cleaning from being an all-out fight with your dog. Brushing a dog's teeth is a little weird, and your Leonberger may not be terribly happy with someone putting stuff in his mouth. However, once he is accustomed to it, the task will likely only take a few minutes a day. Regular brushing keeps down plaque and tartar, making your pup's teeth healthier.

Always use a toothpaste that is made for dogs; human toothpaste can be toxic for your big friend. There are assorted flavors of dog toothpaste, which will make it easier when brushing your Leonberger's teeth, and it could also be entertaining as he tries to eat the meat-flavored toothpaste!

The following are the steps for brushing your dog's teeth:

1. Put a little toothpaste on your finger and hold it out to your dog.

2. Let your dog lick the toothpaste from your finger.

3. Praise your dog for trying something new.

4. Put a little toothpaste on your finger again, lift your dog's upper lip, and begin to rub in circles along your Leonberger's gums. Your pup will likely make it difficult by constantly trying to lick your finger. Give your puppy praise when he doesn't lick the toothpaste or doesn't wiggle too much.

   a. Try to move your finger in a circular motion. This will be very tricky, especially if you have a puppy with sharp baby teeth.

   b. Try to keep the dog still without putting him in a vise. As your puppy gets bigger, he'll need to know how to sit for the cleaning process voluntarily.

5. Try to massage both the top and bottom gums. It is likely the first few times you won't be able to do much more than get your finger in your dog's mouth, and that's okay. Over time, your dog will learn to listen

because general behavioral training will reinforce listening to your commands.

6. Stay positive. No, you probably won't be able to clean your dog's teeth properly for a while, and that is perfectly fine—as long as you keep working at it patiently and consistently.

Once your dog seems comfortable with having his teeth brushed with your finger, try the same steps with a canine toothbrush. (It could take a couple of weeks before you can graduate to this stage.)

Dental Chews

One of the healthiest treats to give any dog is dental chews. While you will need to keep count of the treats as a part of your dog's daily caloric intake, they help with taking care of your dog's teeth. They aren't a replacement for regular brushing, but they are a good complement. Dogs tend to love these treats, and they help improve your dog's breath, so it is a win-win. Make sure to do your research to ensure that you are giving your dog the healthiest dental chews. You don't want to give your Leonberger any treats that have questionable or uncertain ingredients.

CHAPTER 16

General Health Issues: Allergies, Parasites, and Vaccinations

Your Leonberger is pretty much guaranteed to love going outside, which is great if you love to be outdoors. However, going outside means exposing your dog to a lot of allergies and parasites. Odds are that your Leonberger will have allergies, and the problem will present on your dog's skin. And with all that fur, parasites are going to be difficult to find as they will have many places to hide.

Environmental factors largely determine whether or not your dog gets parasites. For example, if you live near a wooded area, your dog is at a greater risk of having ticks than a dog that lives in the city. Fleas are a universal problem for all dogs because fleas can live in any grass, short or long. If you notice rashes or skin irritation, it could be an allergic reaction or symptoms of a parasite. Talk to your vet about all potential environmental risks and any skin conditions you notice when you groom your dog.

Photo Courtesy of Jan Meendering

The Role of Your Veterinarian

Scheduled veterinary visits, routine vaccinations, and regular checkups make for a healthy Leonberger. If your dog seems sluggish or less excited than usual, it could be a sign there is something wrong with him. Fortunately, the breed's personality tends to make it easy to tell when your dog isn't feeling well. Annual visits to the vet will help catch any problems that might be slowly draining the energy or the health from your dog.

Regular checkups also make sure that your Leonberger is aging well. If your dog shows symptoms of a potential problem, an early diagnosis will address the problem. You and your vet can create a plan to manage any pain or problems that come with your dog's aging process. The vet may recommend adjustments to your schedule to accommodate your pup's aging body and his diminishing abilities. This will ensure that the two of you can keep having fun together without hurting your dog.

Vets can provide treatment or preventive medication for parasites and other microscopic threats that your dog might encounter on a daily basis, whether playing outside or when he is exposed to dogs or other animals.

Allergies

A common problem with the Leonberger is allergies – it's far more likely that yours will have them than not, so if you see your dog scratching a lot, there are very good odds the problem is allergies. Dog allergies are usually a result of allergens (such as dust, mold, or pollen), which irritate the skin or nasal passages. Dogs often develop allergies when they are between one and five years old. Once they develop an allergy, canines never outgrow the problem.

The scientific name for environmental allergies is atopic dermatitis. However, it is difficult to know if the problem is environmental or if it is a food you are feeding your dog.

The following symptoms can be seen when either type of allergy is present:

- Itching/scratching, particularly around the face
- Hot spots
- Ear infections
- Skin infections
- Runny eyes and nose (not as common)

Since the symptoms are the same for food and environmental allergies, your vet will help determine the cause. If your dog has a food allergy, change the food that you give him. If he has an environmental allergy, he will need medication, just as humans do. There are several types of medications that can help your dog become less sensitive to allergens:

- Antibacterial/Antifungal – These treatments only address the problems that come with allergies; shampoos, pills, and creams usually do not directly treat the allergy itself.

- Anti-inflammatories – These are over-the-counter medications that are comparable to allergy medicine for people. Don't give your dog any medication without first consulting with the vet. You will need to monitor your dog to see if he has any adverse effects. If your dog is lethargic, has diarrhea, or shows signs of dehydration, consult with your vet immediately.

- Immunotherapy – This is a series of shots that can help reduce your dog's sensitivity to whatever he is allergic to. You can learn from your vet how to give your dog these shots at home. Scientists are also developing an oral version of this medication to make it easier to take care of your dog.

- Topical – This medication is usually a type of shampoo and conditioner that will remove any allergens from your dog's fur. Giving your dog a warm (not hot) bath can also help relieve itching.

To determine the best treatment for your situation, talk with your vet.

Inhalant and Environmental Allergies

Inhalant allergies are caused by things like dust, pollen, mold, and dog dander. Your dog might scratch at a particular hot spot, or he might paw at his eyes and ears. Some dogs have runny noses and sneeze prolifically, in addition to scratching.

Contact Allergies

Contact allergies mean that your dog has touched something that triggers an allergic reaction. Substances like wool, chemicals in a flea treatment, and certain grasses can trigger irritation in a dog's skin, even causing discoloration. If left untreated, the allergic reaction can cause the affected area to emit a strong odor or cause fur loss.

Like food allergies, contact allergies are easy to treat because once you know what is irritating your dog's skin, you can remove the problem.

Fleas and Ticks

Make it a habit to check for ticks after every outing into the woods or near long grass or wild plants. Comb through your dog's fur and check his skin for signs of irritation and for any parasites. Since you will be brushing him several times a week, you should be able to recognize when there's a change, such as a new bump.

Fleas are problematic because they're far more mobile than ticks. The best way to look for fleas is to make it a regular part of your brushing sessions. If you see black specks on the flea comb after brushing through your dog's fur, this could be a sign of fleas.

Instead of using a comb, you can also put your dog on a white towel and run your hand over the fur. Fleas and flea dirt are likely to fall onto the towel. Fleas often are seen on the stomach, so you may notice them when your pup wants a belly rub. You can also look for behavioral indicators, such as incessant scratching and licking. If fleas are a problem, you will need to use flea preventative products on a regular basis once your puppy has reached the appropriate age.

*Photo Courtesy
of Brian and Leah Peters*

Both fleas and ticks can carry parasites and illnesses that can be passed on to you and your family. Ticks carry Lyme disease, which can be debilitating or deadly if untreated. Lyme disease symptoms include headaches, fever, and fatigue. The bite itself often has a red circle around it.

Ticks will fall off your dog once they are full, so if you find a tick on your dog, it will either be looking for a place to latch onto your dog, or it will be feeding. Use the following steps to remove the tick if it has latched onto your dog.

1. Apply rubbing alcohol to the area where the tick is located.

2. Use tweezers to pull the tick off your dog. Do not use your fingers because infections are transmitted through blood, and you don't want the tick to latch onto you.

3. Place the tick in a bag and make sure it is secure so that it does not fall out. The vet can assess the type of tick for diagnostic purposes since different types of ticks carry different diseases.

4. Examine the spot where the tick was to make sure it is fully removed. Sometimes the head will remain under the dog's skin, so make sure all of the tick has been removed.

5. Set up a meeting with the vet to have your dog checked.

The FDA has issued a warning about some store-bought treatments for fleas and ticks. Treatments can be applied monthly, or you can purchase a collar for constant protection. Either way, make sure the treatment does not contain isoxazoline, which can have a negative effect on some pets. (This chemical is found in Bravecto, Nexgard, Credelio, and Simparica.)

Most ingredients in these treatments are safe if the proper dose is used. However, if you use a product that is meant for a larger dog, the effects can be toxic to your smaller dog or not as effective if you use a dosage meant for a smaller dog on your large dog. Consult your vet for recommended treatments and administer the appropriate dose of flea and tick repellant for your dog's size and needs. When you start applying the treatment, watch your dog for the following issues:

- Diarrhea/vomiting
- Trembling
- Lethargy
- Seizures

Take your dog to the vet if you notice any of these issues.

Never use any cat product on a dog and vice versa. If your dog is sick, pregnant, or nursing, you may need to look for an alternative preventative treatment. If you have a cat or young children, you should choose one of the other preventative options for keeping fleas and ticks away. This is because flea collars contain an ingredient that is lethal to felines and which might be carcinogenic to humans.

The packaging on flea treatments will advise you when to begin treating your dog based on his current age and size. Different brands have different recommendations, and you don't want to start treating your puppy too early. There are also important steps to applying the treatment. Make sure you understand all of the steps before purchasing the flea treatment.

If you want to use natural products instead of chemicals, research the alternatives and decide what works best for your Leonberger. Verify that any natural products work before you buy them, and make sure you consult with your vet. Establish a regular monthly schedule and add it to your calendar so that you remember to consistently treat your dog for fleas and ticks.

Parasitic Worms

Although worms are a less common problem than fleas and ticks, they can be far more dangerous. The following lists the types of worms that you should be aware of:

- Heartworms
- Hookworms
- Roundworms
- Tapeworms
- Whipworms

Unfortunately, there isn't an easy-to-recognize set of symptoms to help identify when your dog has worms. However, you can keep an eye out for the following symptoms, and if your dog shows any of these warning signs, schedule a visit to the vet:

- Your Leonberger is unexpectedly lethargic for a few days.
- Patches of fur begin to fall out (this will be noticeable if you brush your Leonberger regularly), or you notice patchy spaces in your dog's coat.
- Your dog's stomach becomes distended (expands) and looks like a potbelly.
- Your Leonberger begins coughing, vomiting, has diarrhea, or has a loss of appetite.

If you aren't sure about any symptom, it's always best to get your dog to the vet as soon as possible.

Heartworms

Heartworms are a significant threat to your dog's health and can be deadly as they can both slow and stop blood flow. As such, you should consistently treat your dog with heartworm protection.

Fortunately, there are medications that prevent your dog from developing heartworms. To prevent this deadly problem, you can give your dog a chewable medication, topical medicine, or you can request shots.

The heartworm parasite is carried by mosquitoes, and it is a condition that is costly and time-consuming to treat. The following are the steps involved in treating your dog for heartworms:

- The vet will draw blood for testing, which can cost as much as $1,000.

- Treatment will begin with some initial medications, including antibiotics and anti-inflammatory drugs.

- Following a month of the initial medication, your vet will give your dog three shots over the course of two months.

From the time of diagnosis until the confirmation your dog is free of heartworms, you will need to be extremely cautious when you exercise your dog because the worms are in your dog's heart, and that inhibits blood flow. This means raising your dog's heart rate too much could kill him. Your vet will tell you how best to exercise your canine during this time. Considering your Leonberger may want to be energetic, this could be a very rough time for both you and your dog.

HELPFUL TIP
Leonberger Health Foundation International (LHFI)

The Leonberger Health Foundation International (LHFI) was founded in 2000 and granted 501(c)(3) status in 2002. This organization aims to collect and distribute funds to support health-related research on the Leonberger breed. Over $460,000 has been raised since 2000 in support of this cause. For the most up-to-date information on research projects funded by LHFI, visit their website at www.lhfi.org.

Treatment will continue after the shots are complete. After approximately six months, your vet will conduct another blood test to ensure the worms are gone.

Once your dog is cleared of the parasites, you will need to begin medicating your dog against heartworms in the future. There will be lasting damage to your dog's heart, so you will need to ensure that your dog does not overexercise.

Intestinal Worms: Hookworms, Roundworms, Tapeworms, and Whipworms

All four of these worms thrive in your dog's intestinal tract, and they get there when your dog eats something contaminated. The following are the most common ways dogs ingest worms:

- Feces
- Small hosts, such as fleas, cockroaches, earthworms, and rodents
- Soil, including licking it from their fur and paws
- Contaminated water
- Mother's milk (If the mother has worms, she can pass them on to young puppies when they nurse.)

The following are the most common symptoms and problems caused by intestinal parasites:

- Anemia
- Blood loss
- Coughing
- Dehydration
- Diarrhea
- Large intestine inflammation
- Weight loss
- A pot-bellied appearance

If a dog lies in soil with hookworm larvae, the parasites can burrow through the canine's skin. Vets will conduct a diagnostic test to determine if your dog has this parasite, and if your dog does have hookworms, the vet will prescribe a dewormer. If your dog is infested with hookworms, you should visit a doctor yourself because humans can get hookworms, too. Being treated at the same time as your Leonberger will help stop the vicious cycle of continually trading off which of you has hookworms.

Roundworms are quite common, and at some point in their lives, most dogs have to be treated for them. The parasites primarily eat the digested food in your dog's stomach, getting the nutrients your dog needs. It is possible for larvae to remain in your dog's stomach even after all of the adult worms have been eradicated. If your Leonberger is pregnant, her puppies should be checked periodically to make sure the inactive larvae are not passed on to the puppies. The mother will also need to go through the same testing to make sure the worms don't make her sick.

Tapeworms are usually eaten when they are eggs and are carried by fleas or from the feces of other animals who also have tapeworms. The eggs develop in the canine's small intestine until they reach the adult stage. Over time, parts of the tapeworm will break off and can be seen in your dog's waste. If this happens, you should be very thorough when cleaning up any waste so other animals will not also contract tapeworms. While tapeworms are not usually fatal, they can cause weight loss and give your dog a potbelly. (The size of your dog's stomach depends on how big the worms grow in your dog's intestines.)

Your vet can test your dog for tapeworms and can prescribe medication to take care of the problem. The medication might include chewable tablets, regular tablets, or a powder that can be sprinkled on your dog's food. There is a minimal risk of humans catching tapeworms, but children are at the greatest risk. Be sure children wash their hands carefully when playing in areas used by your dog. It is also possible to contract tapeworms if a person swallows a flea, which is feasible if your dog and home have a serious infestation.

Whipworms grow in the large intestine, and when in large numbers, they can be fatal. Their name is indicative of the appearance of their tails, which are thinner than their upper section. Like the other worms, you will need to have your dog tested to determine if he has acquired whipworms.

Staying current with flea treatments, properly disposing of your pet's waste, and making sure your Leonberger does not eat trash or animal waste will help prevent your dog from getting these parasites.

Medication to prevent these four parasites can often be included in your dog's heartworm medication. Be sure to speak with your vet regarding the different options.

Photo Courtesy of Alitza Vagenknechtova

Vaccinating Your Leonberger

Vaccination schedules are routine for most dog breeds, including Leonbergers. Make sure to add this information to your calendar, and until your puppy has completed his vaccinations, he should avoid contact with other dogs.

The following list can help you schedule your Leonberger's vaccinations:

Timeline	Shot		
6 to 8 weeks	Bordetella Lyme	Leptospira Influenza Virus-H3N8	DHPP – First shot Influenza Virus-H3N2
10 to 12 weeks	Leptospira Lyme	DHPP – Second Rabies shot Influenza Virus-H3N8	Influenza Virus-H3N2
14 to 16 weeks	DHPP – Third shot		
Annually	Leptospira Lyme	Bordetella Influenza Virus-H3N8	Rabies Influenza Virus-H3N2
Every 3 Years	DHPP Booster	Rabies (if opted for longer duration vaccination)	

These shots protect your dog against a range of ailments. Keep in mind these shots should be a part of your dog's annual vet visit so you can continue to keep your pup safe!

Holistic Alternatives

Wanting to prevent exposure to chemical treatments for your dog makes sense, and there are many good reasons why people are moving to more holistic methods. However, if you decide to go with holistic medication, talk with your vet first about reputable options. You can also seek out Leonberger experts for recommendations before you start trying any holistic methods of care.

It is possible something like massage therapy can help your dog, especially as he ages. Even chiropractic therapy is available for dogs, but you will need to be sure to find a reputable chiropractor for your pup so the treatment doesn't do more harm than good. Follow recommendations on reputable, holistic Leonberger websites to provide the best, safest care for your dog.

CHAPTER 17

Genetic Health Concerns Common to the Leonberger

Generally, Leonbergers are considered a healthy breed, but they do have a few serious ailments and some common ailments. As mentioned in the previous chapter, Leonbergers tend to have allergies. The issues covered in this chapter are more serious and, in many instances, will take greater care to treat.

Common Leonberger Health Issues

You want to make sure that you catch health issues early to improve your dog's quality of life. Take the time to monitor your dog for those potential health problems.

Cataracts

Cataracts are a fairly common problem for all dogs, but considering how much quicker large dogs reach their senior years, you need to be monitoring your Leonberger for this problem far earlier than you do for most other breeds. Cataracts are caused by the lens appearing to be cloudy. Since Leonbergers have a higher risk of cataracts from a young age (it is hereditary in the breed), monitor your dog's eyes for signs of cataracts. Good breeders will have their breeding dogs certified against this kind of problem, but even if your dog doesn't develop hereditary cataracts, there is a very good chance that he will develop cataracts as he ages—most animals do.

In the worst cases, cataracts can cause blindness, though most cataracts cause little to no problem. If you notice your Leonberger's eyes starting to appear cloudy, have your vet check your dog to make sure that the cataracts are not causing your dog problems. Cataracts can be removed surgically, but Leonbergers are sensitive to anesthetics, so you want to avoid unnecessary surgeries.

Bloat/Gastric Dilatation and Volvulus (GDV)

GDV, more commonly known as bloat, is a problem with dog breeds that have larger chests. Their stomach can fill with gases, causing the stomach to bloat. In the worst cases, the gas can cause the stomach to twist, cutting off the entrance and exit from the stomach. Nothing can enter or leave your dog's stomach once the stomach twists. While the bloat stage is not lethal, once the stomach twists, it can kill your dog.

Prevention is the best way of dealing with this problem. While you can have surgery done to keep the stomach from twisting, this may not be the best method of treatment for Leonbergers. You can reduce the risk of this problem by taking the following measures.

- Feed your dog two or three times a day (not just one meal)
- Add wet dog food to kibble (if you feed your dog commercial dog food)
- Ensure the dry dog food is calcium-rich

Hip and Elbow Dysplasia

Hip and elbow dysplasia are common ailments for medium- and larger-sized dogs. Their diet (Chapter 14) as a puppy can help minimize the problem when they are adults. Both types of dysplasia are a result of the dog's hip and leg sockets being malformed, and that often leads to arthritis because the improper fit damages cartilage. The condition is possible to detect by the time a dog becomes an adult. The only way to detect it, though, is through X-rays.

HEALTH ALERT!
Identifying Hip Dysplasia

Hip dysplasia is a common issue seen in many large- and giant-breed dogs. Symptoms may vary but can include:
- Decreased activity
- Stiffness or limping
- Lameness in rear legs
- Difficulty or reluctance to climb stairs, jump, or run

Diagnosis is typically made with an X-ray, and treatment will depend on the severity and cause of the hip dysplasia.

This is a problem that your Leonberger may try to hide because he won't want to slow down. Your adult dog will walk a little more stiffly or may pant even when it's not hot. It usually becomes more obvious as a dog nears his golden years; similar to the way older people tend to change their gait to accommodate pain, your dog may do the same thing. Getting up may be a little more difficult in the beginning and will likely get worse as he ages.

While surgery is an option in severe cases, most dogs can benefit from less invasive treatment:

- Anti-inflammatory medications – Talk to your vet (dogs should not have large doses of anti-inflammatory drugs on a daily basis the way people do since aspirin and anti-inflammatories can damage your dog's kidneys.)

Photo Courtesy
of James and Stephanie Lucero

Photo Courtesy of Angela Cairns

- Lower the amount of high-impact exercise your dog gets, especially on wood floors, tile, concrete, or other hard surfaces. Given how much your dog probably loves to swim, you can move more to a swimming exercise regimen to keep him active without the jarring motions of walking and jogging on hard surfaces.
- Joint fluid modifiers
- Physical therapy
- Weight loss (for dogs who are overweight or obese)

Inherited Polyneuropathy

This is an ailment not found in most other breeds, and the term refers to several potential neuromuscular diseases. Over time, your dog won't be able to continue to get higher levels of exercise and may start to have problems walking, particularly in his back legs. The muscles begin wasting away, affecting his gait, bark, and breathing ability—any muscle can be affected, but it often is most obvious in the back legs and throat. Your dog may not be able to walk as he can no longer support his own weight.

This issue is caused by genetic mutations. Severe cases can be treated with surgery, though the affected part of the body may affect how effective the treatment is. This is why it is important to ensure that breeders do not breed dogs that are carriers of the problem. When a dog starts to show symptoms of the problem (hitches in his gait and changes in his bark), there are usually a limited number of steps that can be taken, and the dog's quality of life will almost always continue to decrease. It is best to talk to a vet to determine the next steps if your dog has this disease.

Leukoencephalomyelopathy

This is a genetic disease that is often covered by guarantees, and no breeder should allow parent dogs to breed who are known to have the genetic defect. The only other breed that is known to have this disease is the Rottweiler.

This is a genetic disorder that affects the central nervous system. Dogs will develop lesions on their spinal cord, causing them to drag their paws as it gets worse. It may not take more than a few months for the dog to become immobile. There is no treatment.

Photo Courtesy
of Jarek Zieliński

Osteochondritis Dessicans

This disease affects the joint areas as cartilage on the bone dies and settles into joints. It occurs more often in a Leonberger's shoulder joints, but it can happen in his hock joints. When the remnants of the cartilage form a little flap that slips into the joint, it can cause discomfort and limping. When these flaps form, surgery is the only way to remove them. There is no way to prevent them, but making sure your Leonberger doesn't suffer injuries to the elbows and other joints can reduce the risks of this problem.

Pano Eosinophilic Panosteitis

This is a problem that happens in humans as well as big dogs, and we commonly call it growing pains. It occurs when the longer bones in the body hurt in young dogs (and people). Dogs may start to limp without any injury occurring, and males are more likely to display this problem than females. The most common age for the problems is between eight and 12 months old. Vets may detect the problem using X-rays, and usually, an anti-inflammatory is given to help manage the pain.

Since this problem is literally about the growth process, some vets may have you try to better manage the growth process. Over time, your dog will get over the problem as the bones finish growing, and the condition does not have any associated long-term effects. However, it is still important to monitor your young dog for this problem and to make sure that you are keeping him from feeling significant pain. Limping can also be a sign of an injury, so you want to make sure that you know what is causing your dog to limp in case it is something serious.

Perianal Fistulas

This is a disease that affects the area around the anus and is not just a problem in dogs. Perianal fistulas are mostly found in German Shepherds, but they are also known to occur in some Leonbergers (and other dog breeds). The perianal area is just around the anus, or the location where the digestive tract ends. The problem occurs when an infection starts in the area, resulting in draining tracts.

Usually, the problem is found during regular checks (and this is why checks are so important) as the early signs are usually too innocuous to see. When the problem gets worse, the dog may have a harder time doing his business, and blood may appear in his feces. The dog may also lose his appetite and try to lick the area increasingly often. When it gets bad, your dog may not even want to sit because of the discomfort, or he may get aggressive or depressed. This is more likely to be a problem in males than in females, especially if the male has not been fixed.

Until recently, the most recommended treatment was surgery, but a few drugs have been developed that are now more commonly recommended. Your dog is likely to see some rapid improvement in the early days of treatment, but you need to keep the treatment going to ensure that the problem remains under control. In the worst situation, surgery may still be required. It is also possible that treatment will be required on and off for the rest of your dog's life, depending on how severe the case is. The ailment is not fatal, but it can be incredibly painful and uncomfortable, though it is something that is always treatable.

Common Owner Mistakes

"

Keep your Leo slim. Often people do not take into account the treats they are giving the dog and then feed it without considering the treats. As with any giant breed, being overweight causes all kinds of health issues.

BRENDA FORD & MARY ANN FARENZENA
Leos from the Lion's Den

"

In addition to genetic problems, there are things you can do that could unintentionally damage your dog's health; these mistakes are related to diet and exercise levels. In the puppy stage, it is a difficult balance to strike as your puppy is curious and enthusiastic. Even when he is a fully grown dog, you have to make sure you are minimizing how much stress is placed on your Leonberger's body. Weight management is one important way of keeping your dog healthy. You need to balance your dog's diet with his level of activity to prevent exacerbation of hip and elbow dysplasia.

Failing to notice early signs of potential issues can be detrimental or even fatal to your Leonberger. Any changes in your Leonberger's behavior are likely a sign of something that should be checked by your vet.

Prevention and Monitoring

Checking your Leonberger's weight is important and should be done at least once a quarter or twice a year. You and your vet should keep an eye on your dog's weight, as being overweight puts a strain on your dog's back, legs, joints, and muscles.

CHAPTER 18

The Aging Leonberger

It's sad, but the Leonberger's average life span is only between eight and nine years. Some sources do report a low end of seven years, and others a high end of 10 years, making it very worth your while to ask breeders if they know roughly how long their dogs tend to live. You may start to notice your dog slowing down between the ages of five and seven years. A dog may remain healthy his whole life, but his body still won't be able to do the same activities during the later years that he could do easily at two. For larger dogs, the decline often seems to happen a lot faster. The first signs are usually your dog's walking becoming a little stiffer or when he starts panting more heavily earlier in the walk or jog. If you see any of these signs, start to tone back the jogs or stop jogging and just go for more energetic walks. It's likely that your Leonberger will want to continue to exercise as he ages, so you will need to either choose easier walks or start to include your dog in other kinds of activities.

Your schedule is going to need to change as your canine slows down. Be careful to ensure that your pup doesn't overexert himself, as Leonbergers may be too focused on being active to realize they're hurting and need to stop to rest.

There is a reason these are called the golden years—you can really enjoy them with your dog. You don't have to worry as

HELPFUL TIP
Do Leonbergers Age Faster?

In the animal kingdom, larger animals typically live longer than their smaller counterparts, but this, unfortunately, doesn't hold true for animals within a species. Larger dogs age much faster than small dogs. Leonbergers live an average of seven to nine years, but it's nearly impossible to predict how long your Leonberger will live. Preventative health care, including regular checkups, combined with a healthy diet and regular exercise, are the best ways to ensure your dog lives a long, happy life.

much about him tearing things up out of boredom or getting overexcited on walks anymore. You can enjoy lazy evenings and peaceful weekends with some less strenuous exercise to break up the day. It's easy to make the senior years incredibly enjoyable for your Leonberger and yourself by making the necessary adjustments.

Senior Care Challenges

In most cases, caring for an older dog is much simpler than taking care of a younger dog, and Leonbergers are no exception.

Accommodations you should make for your senior Leonberger include:

- Set water bowls out in a couple of different places so that your dog can easily reach them as needed. If your Leonberger shows signs of having trouble drinking or eating, place slightly raised water dishes around the home.

- Cover hard floor surfaces (such as tile, hardwood, and vinyl). Use nonslip carpets or rugs.

- Add cushions and softer bedding for your Leonberger. This will both make the surface more comfortable and help him stay warmer. There are bed warmers for dogs if your Leonberger has achy joints or muscles. Of course, you also need to make sure he isn't too warm, so this can be a fine balancing act.

- To improve his circulation, increase how often you brush your Leonberger.

- Stay inside in extreme heat and cold. Your Leonberger is hardy, but an old canine cannot handle extreme changes as well as he once did.

- Use stairs or ramps for your Leonberger wherever possible so that the old pup doesn't have to try to jump.

- Avoid moving your furniture around, particularly if your Leonberger shows signs of having trouble with his sight or has dementia. A familiar home is more comforting and less stressful as your pet ages. If your Leonberger isn't able to see as clearly as he once did, keeping the home familiar will make it easier for your dog to move around without getting hurt.

- If you have stairs, consider setting up an area where your dog can stay without having to go up and down too often.

- Create a space where your Leonberger can relax with fewer distractions and noises. Don't make your old friend feel isolated, but do give him a place to get away from everyone if he needs to be alone.

- Be prepared to let your dog out more often for restroom breaks.

Common Physical Disorders Related to Aging

Chapters 4 and 16 cover illnesses that are common or likely with a Leonberger, but old age tends to bring a slew of ailments that aren't particular to any one breed. Here are the things you will need to watch for (as well as talking to your vet about them).

- Diabetes is probably the greatest concern for a breed that loves to eat as much as your Leonberger does, even with two hours of daily exercise most of the dog's adult life. Although diabetes is usually thought of as a genetic condition, any Leonberger can become diabetic if not fed and exercised properly. This is another reason why it's so important to be careful with your Leonberger's diet and exercise levels.

- Arthritis is probably the most common ailment in any dog breed, and the Leonberger is no exception. If your dog is showing signs of stiffness and pain after normal activities, talk with your vet about safe ways to help minimize the pain and discomfort of this common joint ailment.

- Gum disease is a common issue in older dogs as well, and you should be just as vigilant about brushing his teeth when your dog gets older as at any other age. A regular check of your Leonberger's teeth and gums can help ensure this does not become a problem.

- Loss of eyesight or blindness is relatively common in older dogs, just as it is in humans. Have your dog's vision checked at least once a year and more often if it is obvious that his eyesight is failing.

- Kidney disease is a common problem in older dogs and one that you should monitor for the older your Leonberger gets. If

Photo Courtesy of Lavinia Virgo

your canine is drinking more often and having accidents regularly, get your Leonberger to the vet as soon as possible and have him checked for kidney disease.

Steps, Ramps, and Wheelchairs

You shouldn't pick your large Leonberger up to carry him upstairs or put him in the car. Steps and ramps are the best way to safely ensure your Leonberger can maintain some level of self-sufficiency as he ages. Also, using steps and ramps provides a bit of extra exercise.

Vet Visits

As your Leonberger ages, you are going to notice the slowdown, and the pains in your Leonberger's body are going to be obvious, just like they are in an older person. You need to make sure that you have regular visits with your vet to ensure that you aren't doing anything that could potentially harm your Leonberger. If your Leonberger has a debilitating ailment or condition, you may want to discuss the options for ensuring a better quality of life, such as wheels if your Leonberger's legs begin to have serious issues. In the worst cases, you may want to discuss the quality of your Leonberger's life with the vet.

The Importance of Regular Vet Visits

Just as humans go to visit the doctor more often as they age, you'll need to take your dog to see your vet with greater frequency. The vet can make sure that your Leonberger is staying active without overdoing it and that there is no unnecessary stress on your older dog. If your canine has sustained an injury and hidden it from you, your vet is more likely to detect it.

Your vet can also make recommendations about activities and changes to your schedule based on your Leonberger's physical abilities and any changes in personality. For example, if your Leonberger is panting more now, it could be a sign of pain from stiffness. This could be difficult to distinguish given how much Leonbergers pant as a rule, but if you see other signs of pain, schedule a visit with the vet. Your vet can help you determine the best way to keep your Leonberger happy and active during the later years.

What to Expect at Vet Visits

- Your vet is going to talk about your dog's history, even if you have visited every year. This talk is necessary to see how things have gone or if any possible problems have started to show or have gotten worse.
- While you chat, your vet will probably conduct a complete physical examination to assess your dog's health.
- Depending on how old your dog is and the kind of health he is in, your vet may want to run different tests. The following are some of the most common tests for older dogs.
  - Arthropod-borne disease testing, which involves drawing blood and testing it for viral infections
  - Chemistry screening for kidney, liver, and sugar evaluation
  - Complete blood count
  - Fecal flotation, which involves mixing your dog's poop with a special liquid to test for worms and other parasites
  - Heartworm testing
  - Urinalysis, which tests your dog's urine to check the health of your dog's kidneys and urinary system
- The same routine wellness check that the vet has been conducting on your dog all his life
- Any breed-specific tests for your aging Leonberger

Changes to Watch for

> *I try to keep my dogs active even in their senior years. Obviously, the length of our walks and training sessions is much shorter, but the physical activity is good for keeping your Leo's joints mobile, and the mental stimulation of training keeps up his cognitive function. I encourage joint support supplements, and you may need to look at alternative health support such as chiropractic and acupuncture to keep your aging Leo more comfortable and mobile.*
>
> ERIN ANDERSEN
> *High Hopes Newfoundlands and Leonbergers*

Photo Courtesy
of Maria Wallace

Keep an eye out for different signs that your dog is slowing down. This will help you to know when to adjust the setup around your home and to reduce how much your old pup is exercising.

Appetite and Nutritional Requirements

With less exercise, your dog doesn't need as many calories, which means you need to adjust your pup's diet. If you opt to feed your Leonberger commercial dog food, make sure you change to a senior food. Senior food is designed for the changing dietary needs of older dogs, with fewer calories and more nutrients that the older dog body needs.

If you make your Leonberger's food, talk to your vet and take the time to research how best to reduce calories without sacrificing taste. Your canine is going to need less fat in his food, so you may need to find something healthier that still has a lot of taste to supplement the types of foods you gave your Leonberger as a puppy or active adult dog.

Exercise

Since Leonbergers are so gregarious, they are going to be just as happy with extra attention from you as they were with exercise when they were younger. If you make fewer demands, decrease the number of walks, or in any way change the routine, your Leonberger will quickly adapt to the new program. You will need to make those changes based on your dog's ability, so it's up to you to adjust the schedule and keep your Leonberger happily active. Shorter, more frequent walks should take care of your Leonberger's exercise needs, as well as help to break up your day a little more.

Your dog will enjoy napping as much as walking, especially if he gets to cuddle with you. Sleeping beside you while you watch television or as you yourself nap is pretty much all it takes to make your older Leonberger content, but he still needs to exercise.

The way your Leonberger slows down will probably be the hardest part of watching him age. You may notice that your Leonberger spends more time sniffing during walks, which could be a sign that your dog is tiring. It could also be his way of acknowledging that long steady walks are a thing of the past, and so he is stopping to enjoy the little things more. Stopping to smell things may now give him the excitement that he used to get by walking farther.

While you should be watching for your dog to tire, he may also let you know. If he is walking slower, looking up at you, and flopping down, that could be his way of letting you know it's time to return home. If your canine can't manage long walks, make the walks shorter and more numerous and spend more time romping around your yard or home with your buddy.

Aging and the Senses

Just like people, dogs' senses weaken as they get older, and larger dogs' senses tend to deteriorate faster than smaller dogs. They won't hear things as well as they used to, they won't see things as clearly, and their sense of smell will weaken.

The following are some of the signs that your dog is losing at least one of his senses.

- It becomes easy to surprise or startle your dog. You need to be careful because this can make your Leonberger aggressive, a scary prospect even in old age. Do NOT sneak up on your old dog, as this can be bad for both of you, and he deserves better than to be scared.

- Your dog may seem to ignore you because he is less responsive when you issue a command. If you have not had a problem before, your dog isn't being stubborn; he is likely losing his hearing.

- Cloudy eyes may be a sign of loss of sight, though it does not mean that your dog is blind.

If your dog seems to be "behaving badly," it is a sign that he is aging, not that he doesn't care or wants to rebel. Do not punish your older dog.

Adjust your schedule to meet your dog's changing abilities. Adjust water bowl height, refrain from rearranging rooms, and pet your dog more often. He is probably nervous about losing his abilities, so it is up to you to comfort him.

Keeping Your Senior Dog Mentally Active

Just because your Leonberger can't walk as far doesn't mean that his brain isn't just as focused and capable. As he slows down physically, focus more on activities that are mentally stimulating. As long as your Leonberger has all of the basics down, you can teach him all kinds of low-impact tricks. At this point, training could be easier because your Leonberger has learned to focus better, and he'll be happy to have something he can still do with you.

New toys are another great way to help keep your dog's mind active. Be careful that the toys aren't too rough on your dog's older jaw and teeth. Tug of war may be a game of the past (you don't want to hurt old teeth), but other games such as hide-and-seek will still be very much appreciated. Whether you hide toys or yourself, this can be a game that keeps your Leonberger guessing. There are also food balls, puzzles, and other games that focus on cognitive abilities.

Some senior dogs suffer from cognitive dysfunction (CCD) syndrome, a type of dementia. It is estimated that 85% of all cases of dementia in dogs go undiagnosed because of the difficulty in pinpointing the problem. It manifests more as a problem of temperament.

If your dog begins to act differently, you should take him to the vet to see if he has CCD. While there really isn't any treatment for it, your vet can recommend things you can do to help your dog. Things like rearranging the rooms of your home are strongly discouraged, as familiarity with his surroundings will help your dog feel more comfortable and will reduce stress as he loses his cognitive abilities. Mental stimulation will help to fight CCD, but you should plan to keep your dog mentally stimulated regardless of whether or not he exhibits symptoms of dementia.

Advantages to the Senior Years

The last years of your Leonberger's life can be just as enjoyable (if not more so) than the earlier stages since your dog has mellowed. All of those high-energy activities will give way to cuddles and relaxing. Having your pup just enjoy your company can be incredibly nice (just remember to keep up his activity levels instead of getting too complacent with your Leonberger's newfound love of resting and relaxing).

Your Leonberger will continue to be a loving companion, interacting with you at every opportunity—that does not change with age. Your canine's limitations should dictate interactions and activities. If you are busy, make sure you schedule time with your Leonberger to do things that are within those limitations. It is just as easy to make an older Leonberger happy as it is with a young one, and it is easier on you since relaxing is more essential to your old friend.

Preparing to Say Goodbye

This is something that all dog parents (well, pet parents really) don't want to think about, but as you watch your Leonberger slow down, you will know that your time with your sweet pup is coming to an end. Most working dogs tend to suddenly decline, making it very obvious when you need to start taking extra care of their aging bodies. They have trouble on smoother surfaces or can't walk nearly as far as they once did. It's certainly sad, but when it starts to happen, you know to begin to prepare to say goodbye.

Some dogs can continue to live for years after they begin to slow down, but most working dogs don't make it more than about a year or two. Sometimes dogs will lose their interest in eating, will have a stroke, or other problem that arises with little warning. Eventually, it will be time to say goodbye, whether at home or at the vet's office. You need to be prepared, and that is exactly why you should be making the most of these last few years.

Talk to your family about how you will care for your dog over the last few years or months of his life. Many dogs will be perfectly happy, despite their limited abilities. Some may begin to have problems controlling their bowel movements, while others may have problems getting up from a prone position. There are solutions to all of these problems. It is key to remember that quality of life should be the primary consideration, and since your dog cannot tell you how he feels, you will have to take cues from your dog. If your dog still seems happy, there is no reason to euthanize him.

At this stage, your dog is probably perfectly happy just sleeping near you for 18 hours a day. That is fine as long as he still gets excited about walking, eating, and being petted. The purpose of euthanasia is to reduce suffering, not to make things more convenient for yourself. This is what makes the decision so difficult, but your dog's behavior should be a fairly good indicator of how he is feeling. Here are some other things to watch to help you evaluate your dog's quality of life:

- Appetite
- Drinking
- Urinating and defecation
- Pain (noted by excessive panting)
- Stress levels
- Desire to be active or with family (if your dog wants to be alone most of the time, that is usually a sign that he is trying to be alone for the end)

Talk to your vet if your dog has a serious illness to determine what the best path forward is. They can provide the best information on the quality of your dog's life and how long your dog is likely to live with the disease or ailment.

*Photo Courtesy
of Lili Costagliola*

If your dog gets to the point when you know that he is no longer happy, he can't move around, or he has a fatal illness, it is probably time to say goodbye. This is a decision that should be made as a family, always putting the dog's needs and quality of life first. If you decide it is time to say goodbye, determine who will be present at the end.

Once at the vet's office, if you have decided to euthanize the dog, you can make the last few minutes very happy by feeding your dog the things that he couldn't eat before. Things like chocolate and grapes can put a smile on his face for the remaining time he has.

You can also have your dog euthanized at home. If you decide to request a vet to come to your home, be prepared for additional charges for the home visit. You also need to determine where you want your dog to be, whether inside or outside, and in which room if you decide to do it inside.

Make sure at least one person is present so that your dog is not alone during the last few minutes of his life. You don't want your dog to die surrounded by strangers. The process is fairly peaceful, but your dog will probably be a little stressed. He will pass within a few minutes of the injection. Continue to talk to him as his brain will continue to work even after his eyes close.

Once your dog is gone, you need to determine what to do with the body.

- Cremation is one of the most common ways of taking care of the body. You can get an urn or request a container to scatter your dog's ashes over his favorite places. Make sure you don't dump his ashes in places where that is not permitted. Private cremation is more expensive than communal cremation, but it means that the only ashes you get are from your dog. Communal creation occurs when several pets are cremated together.

- Burial is the easiest method if you have your pet euthanized at home, but you need to check your local regulations to ensure that you can bury your dog at home, as this is illegal in some places. You also need to consider the soil. If your yard is rocky or sandy, that will create problems with trying to bury your pet at home. Also, don't bury your pet in your yard if it is near wells that people use as a drinking source or if it is near wetlands or waterways. Your dog's body can contaminate the water as it decays. You can also look into a pet cemetery if there is one in your area.

Grief and Healing

Dogs become members of our families, so their passing can be incredibly difficult. People go through all of the same emotions and feelings of loss with a dog as they do with close friends and family. The absence of that presence in your life is jarring, especially with such a loving, loyal dog like the Leonberger. Your home is a constant reminder of the loss, and in the beginning, you and your family will probably feel considerable grief. Saying goodbye is going to be difficult. Taking a couple of days off work is not a bad idea. While people who don't have dogs will say that your Leonberger was just a dog, you know better, and it is okay to feel the pain and to grieve as you would for any lost loved one.

Losing your Leonberger is also going to make a substantial change in your schedule. It will likely take a while to get accustomed to the way your schedule has shifted. Fight the urge to go out and get a new dog because you almost certainly are not ready yet.

Everyone grieves differently, so you will need to allow yourself to grieve in a way that is healthy for you. Everyone in your family will feel the loss differently, too, so let them feel it in their own ways. Some people don't require much time, while others can feel the loss for months. There is no timetable, so you can't try to force it on yourself or any member of your family.

Talk about how you would like to remember your pup and make sure to listen. You can have a memorial for your lost pet, tell stories, and plant a tree in your dog's memory. If someone doesn't want to participate, that is fine.

Try to return to your normal routine as much as possible if you have other pets. This can be both painful and helpful as your other pets will still need you just as much (especially other dogs who have also lost their companion).

If you find that grief is hindering your ability to function normally, seek professional help. If needed, you can go online to find support groups in your area to help you and your family, especially if this was your first dog. Sometimes it helps to talk about the loss so that you can start to heal.

Made in the USA
Coppell, TX
11 October 2022